50 Tax-Smart Investing Strategies

50 Tax-Smart Investing Strategies

And Other Financial Tips To Maximize Your After-Tax Returns And Net Worth

Kurt Rosentreter, C. A.

Stoddart

Published in 1998 by Stoddart Publishing Co. Limited
34 Lesmill Road, Toronto, Canada M3B 2T6
Toll-free tel. for Ontario and Quebec 1-800-387-0141
Toll-free tel. for all other provinces and territories 1-800-287-0172
Fax (416) 445-5967
Email Customer.Service@ccmailgw.genpub.com

02 01 00 99 98 1 2 3 4 5

Canadian Cataloguing in Publication Data
Rosentreter, Kurt
50 tax-smart investing strategies: and other financial planning tips to maximize your after-tax returns and net worth

ISBN 0-7737-5951-4

1. Finance, Personal — Canada. 2. Saving and investment — Canada.
I. Title. II. Title: Fifty tax-smart investing strategies.

HG179.R678 1998 332.024'00971 C97-932548-X

All characters and events in this book's examples are fictitious, and any resemblance to actual persons, living or dead, or actual events is purely coincidental.

Cover design: Pekoe Jones
Text design: Tannice Goddard
Typesetting: Kinetics Design & Illustration

Printed and bound in Canada

CONTENTS

Tax-Smart Investing Strategies: Investment Income

Tax-Smart Investing Strategies: Other Investments

More Tax-Smart Strategies

PREFACE

As the next century approaches, all Canadians are trying to make their incomes go further as they fight rising costs of living, shrinking health-care coverage, and ever-increasing taxes. Separately, focusing on higher investment returns and lower taxes are effective ways to stretch incomes. But the combination of the two, called "tax-smart investing" or thinking about investing on an after-tax basis, can provide Canadians with a powerful tool for growing net worth and improving cash flow.

This book, by focusing on tax-smart investing, takes investing to a new level of thinking. Tax-smart investing means investing with taxes in mind *before* you buy. When you examine the Canadian marketplace for investment products, you will find many investment salespeople selling a broad array of investments, trying to produce the highest possible total return. Most investors, however, measure return on investment by the amount of money in their pockets at the end of the year as compared to the beginning of the year. This means *after-tax*. In this book, I will try to teach you to think more on an after-tax basis, and to educate you about investments and tax, and how to put them together effectively to maximize your after-tax returns.

As Canadians look to the financial marketplace for their investing needs, many are overwhelmed by the choice between thousands of investment products and thousands of people selling investments. This book feels for you as you succumb to investment- and financial-planning information overload in the Canadian marketplace today. This guide will not tell you to "save for retirement." It will not cover the A-to-Zs of financial planning. This book provides 50 strategies designed to assist you in growing your net worth. To-the-point advice for busy Canadians who already have a basic understanding of personal finance.

The strategies presented here are not a comprehensive list, but rather serve as a starting point for examining how to maximize your personal net worth using a variety of techniques. Many of the strategies will require implementation assistance from an investment advisor, financial planner, or income tax specialist. Please consult a professional advisor for advice on how these strategies can be applied to your personal situation. To help you decide who to trust as your advisor, this book also contains some practical tips for evaluating advisor alternatives.

You should also bear in mind that the strategies in this book are based on an understanding of current and drafted income tax legislation. The Minister of Finance can make changes to the Income Tax Act of Canada at any time, and such changes could have a significant impact on these strategies and their applicability to your personal situation. A professional advisor will be able to determine the impact of any changes in tax legislation that occur after the publishing of this book, and should be consulted to determine the applicability of these strategies to your personal situation.

Each of the following 50 strategies is coupled with an

example to illustrate the investment techniques being discussed. You can also follow along in many of the strategies as I "crunch the numbers" to give you a sense of the real savings that can be achieved with tax-smart investing. For the sake of simplicity, I make one or two basic assumptions with the calculations: a rate of 50% is used to represent taxation of regular income in the highest tax bracket in Canada; and unless otherwise stated, dividends are Canadian-sourced dividends that qualify for tax-advantaged treatment in Canada when taxed in an individual's hands.

I have also included a glossary of financial terms to help you as you read these strategies. If you see a word or phrase in italics and are not sure what the term means, you can look it up at the back of the book.

Finally, you will notice that I have deliberately avoided referring to real financial products and companies in this book. Here's why. There are many good investment and insurance products sold and serviced by many highly qualified professional advisors in Canada. But you will have specific needs which should be served by specific solutions. It would be misleading for me to suggest that one particular product fits everyone's personal situation. Instead, I have chosen to provide concepts and strategies around which products can be added.

Take the concepts described in these strategies and, alone or with your financial advisor, seek the product solutions in the marketplace that apply these concepts and address your financial needs and objectives. I hope that you achieve the same value from these strategies that many of my clients already have.

INTRODUCTION

What Is Tax-Smart Investing?

Tax-smart investing is investing to maximize the after-tax return on investments. It means maximizing what you earn, after paying income taxes.

Achieving the after-tax rate of return you desire when you invest is a function of two related factors: buying an investment product that achieves a certain total rate of return; and paying the income tax on the total return earned by the investment product. Many investors and advisors focus only on the investment product when they invest, and neglect to consider the tax impact on their total rate of return. Remember, the interest income, dividends, and capital gains that you include on your tax return, and the tax you pay on this income, affect your rates of return on your taxable investments. The tax paid on this investment income reduces the overall return or profitability of an investment product.

You need to look at the total picture, including taxation, to get a sense of how well you are doing with your investments. Failure to consider the tax effects of investing may result in misleading returns, as a large slice of tax may be taken from the total returns earned.

Tax-smart investing is about minimizing and/or deferring the income tax paid on investment earnings in order to maximize after-tax returns. And tax-smart investing is about implementing other tax-smart strategies across your financial needs spectrum, integrating all areas of financial planning to maximize your total personal net worth.

Over any individual's lifetime, there is probably no greater expenditure made than taxes. Given this, it is in everyone's best interest to implement as many tax-saving and tax-deferral strategies as possible.

To utilize tax-smart investing strategies, investors and their advisors must understand the taxation of the different investment products available today. Additionally, investors and their advisors should understand the investor's marginal tax rate, and marginal tax rate of the investor's spouse and children. We will examine how to do this in the first strategy.

Tax: Only Part of Proper Investment Planning

Tax-smart strategies should be contemplated in the context of your overall investment strategy. The tax effectiveness of investing is only one factor to consider when investing, and investing should not be contemplated for tax reasons alone. Other factors to consider when investing include, but are not limited to, investment performance expectations and needs, investor risk tolerance, investment diversification, current investment holdings, and liquidity needs.

Investors should consult their own professional financial advisors before implementing any of the strategies that follow. The applicability of these 50 strategies to any individual will depend on that individual's personal situation, including tax, financial, legal, and investment characteristics. Investors and their advisors should also evaluate the impact of future changes to the Income Tax Act and other statutes and the impact of these changes to their planning strategies.

Sorting Out Who Your Advisor Should Be

In the last few years, the number of people advising investors about issues of personal finance has exploded in Canada. Consequently, from an investor's point of view, it is becoming more and more difficult to determine who to trust with your money.

Today, standards are developing to regulate financial planners and other advisors in Canada; currently, however, anyone can call him- or herself a financial planner. The population of mutual fund agents, brokers, and other investment salespeople has exploded recently, resulting in some people with little relevant experience or qualifications knocking at your door to sell you investments or insurance.

The following list of characteristics is designed to provide you with guidelines when you sit down with a potential financial advisor. Ask all potential advisors about these characteristics and compare the results before settling on one or a few advisors. Remember, the number and variety of service and product providers in Canada is large, so always compare solutions suggested by several providers to get the best products and services and the fairest cost. This is your life savings, so spend the time to find the properly qualified people to manage it!

Assess potential financial advisors using at least the following considerations:

- Professional qualifications — Don't rush to be impressed by a whack of credentials on someone's business card. There are many designations that individuals may hold that have little to do with what they are consulting you on. Whether it is providing financial-planning services or selling insurance or investments, each area has some form of national association governing its certified members. Contact these national associations and ask questions about what the credentials mean. Ask the associations if these are the best credentials to have for what their members are consulting on. And ask if they are easy credentials to get. Give far more respect to a three-year, six-course program with examinations than to a three-month correspondence course.

- Ongoing professional development — Good professionals and their associations recognize the need to regularly update an advisor's financial knowledge year after year as tax rules change, new investments develop, and so on. Ask your advisors how much formal annual education they are required to have by their association. Look for at least 15 hours.
- Related work experience — In Canada today, you may come across a financial planner or investment advisor who last year was a teacher or a security guard. Just as you want the brightest, most experienced doctor to deal with your physical health, find the most qualified advisor and financial planner to deal with your financial health. After all, it is your financial future we are talking about! Question advisors about how long they have been directly involved in what they are consulting you on. Ask how long they have had their professional qualifications. Look for a minimum of three years of relevant experience. Ask for current clients you can call for an opinion of the advisor.
- Customer-service emphasis: access to advisor, frequency of meetings with you, number of clients — Many advisors today have several hundred clients and counting. Some institutions are restricting the number of clients per advisor in order to maintain a minimum level of customer service. Ask your advisor how often you can meet annually, whether he or she will review your investment

performance with you regularly, and whether he or she will take the time to educate you about what you are buying.

- One-stop shopping — Beware advisors who try to be everything you want but are not appropriately qualified to do so. For example, beware an investment advisor who lectures you on specific tax-saving strategies or rushes to sell you a tax shelter. Unless the advisor is qualified to consult in tax, take your tax needs to a qualified tax professional. Even with these professionals, question them as to their experience in your particular tax area of concern before engaging them.
- Access to all products — It is important that your financial advisor have access to the entire spectrum of investments in order to meet your investment asset allocation needs and your insurance needs. For life insurance, this can mean an advisor having access to term, permanent, and universal life insurance. For investments, this can mean having access to bonds, stripped bonds, TIPS, segregated money management, tax shelters, pooled funds, and so on. As individuals get older, their investment needs change, their risk tolerances change, and their wealth grows. Investors should be exposed to products that best serve their needs over time, and very often this means far more investments than mutual funds and GICs alone.
- Reporting capabilities — Investors want to know their personal annual rates of return on investments in order to know how well they have done. Find advisors who will do this for you, because this is what you need to know to judge their performance. More than that, find advisors who will also compare your personal rate of return to a relevant benchmark like the TSE 300. An advisor who earns you 20% a year on an equity fund, when the TSE 300 earns 28% in the same year, is an underperformer if your goal is to maximize returns. But you may never

know whether the advisor is an underperformer if he or she doesn't show you!

- Objective versus biased advice — In Canada, most investment advisors provide advice and hope to sell you a product to fill the need. When they offer you product choices, in many cases they earn commissions on these products. These commissions may vary by product. In such cases, you never know if the product they sell you is truly what you need or is simply the product that pays the biggest commission to the advisor. Some advisors now charge one fee for all services and say this makes them unbiased. But they may be biased nevertheless if they restrict your investment choice to a small group of products that are offered by their company only. Objectivity means offering choice from the wide range of products available and not receiving a fee from the sale of a product. This is how fee-based advisors operate. They provide you with peace of mind that the advice given is completely in your best interest. These advisors charge a fee for services that they provide. This means that you must put a value on objectivity when deciding what type of advisor to use.
- Comfort factor — Above all, you should be comfortable with your advisor. You should be comfortable approaching the advisor with questions, you should understand the answers, and you should be satisfied that your finances are being handled truly in your best interest and with the utmost professionalism. However, this does not mean that you should invest your life savings with your brother-in-law or your friend from university. Separate personal relations from business and keep emotions out of it. Find an independent advisor who provides you with a comfortable feeling and can also keep an objective eye on your finances.

STRATEGY # 1

Know Your Marginal Tax Rate

Your *marginal tax rate* is the tax rate applicable to the next dollar of *taxable income* you earn. The Canadian tax system uses progressive tax rates, whereby the rate of tax increases as taxable income increases, up to a certain point. Marginal rates of tax vary according to province or territory of residence in Canada, and according to type of income. Understanding marginal tax rates can help you to understand tax paid on incremental income and how that tax may differ according to the nature of the income.

Knowing your own marginal tax rate is important in order to plan how to minimize the tax you pay on additional income. Also, knowing the marginal tax rates of different income types permits you to reduce taxes paid, by varying your investment income mix.

Understanding Taxation of Income Types

Different types of income attract different levels of taxation. Therefore, one of your considerations when buying investments should be the amount of taxes you are going to pay on the type of income earned. The types of income you can earn include *regular income* from business or employment, and *investment income*, including *interest, rent, dividends*, and *capital gains*. Regular income, along with interest income, is the most highly taxed income type. Interest income is earned from bank accounts and from fixed income investments like Canada Savings Bonds, guaranteed investment certificates (*GICs*), and government *Treasury bills*.

Dividends are *distributions* of after-tax income paid by *corporations* to their shareholders. You may receive dividends from the mutual funds you own, if the funds own shares of corporations that pay dividends. Canadian dividends (or simply "dividends") generally attract the least amount of tax among all income types.

Capital gains result when you sell an asset for more than its purchase price. The increase in value is a capital gain, and 75% of the gain (called a *taxable capital gain*) is included in your personal income for tax purposes. Capital gains generally attract more tax than dividends but less than interest and regular income. There are two types of capital gains: *realized* and *unrealized*. An unrealized capital gain consists of the *accrued capital gain* on an asset before the asset is sold or deemed sold. A realized gain generally results when the asset is sold or deemed sold.

Note that interest income earned is usually taxable annually, whether it is received or not. Capital gains, however, are taxable only when realized; that means you may be able to own an investment that has a growing market value and not trigger any tax until it is sold.

Why Knowing Your Marginal Tax Rate Is Important

Knowing your marginal tax rate permits you to calculate the *after-tax rate of return* on additional investment income. It also permits you to calculate the tax savings on your *registered retirement savings plan* (RRSP) deductions. This knowledge may affect the way you decide to invest your money. Since we all care about what goes into our pockets after-tax, having an understanding of the rates is important to us all.

Below I have approximated the marginal tax rates for different taxable income levels in Canada (combined federal and provincial rates). Keep in mind that each province has its own exact rate, which differs from those presented here. For our purposes, however, these approximations are reasonable.

Taxable Income Level	Interest & Regular Income	Dividends	Capital Gains
$6,457 to $29,590	27%	8%	20%
$29,591 to $59,180	43%	27%	32%
$59,181 to $62,195	48%	32%	36%
Greater than $62,195	50%	34%	38%

Here is an approximation of the marginal tax rates on different types of income for someone with taxable income of $30,000 a year:

An additional $1 of interest or regular income would be taxed at a rate of 43%.

An additional $1 of dividend income would be taxed at a rate of 27%.

An additional $1 of capital gains would be taxed at a rate of 32%.

For an individual with a taxable income of $70,000 a year or more,

An additional $1 of interest or regular income would be taxed at a rate of 50%.

An additional $1 of dividend income would be taxed at a rate of 34%.

An additional $1 of capital gains would be taxed at a rate of 38%.

▼

Example

Evelyn is an employee in Ontario who earned $33,000 of taxable income in 1996. She hopes to climb the company ladder quickly and anticipates that her salary will rise rapidly. When it came time to make her *RRSP contribution* for 1996, Evelyn wanted the most bang for her RRSP buck. She reviewed her marginal tax rate and income level, and learned that she had just moved into a higher tax bracket by approximately $3,500 ($33,000 taxable income less $29,500 taxable income threshold from the above table). According to the above marginal income tax rate chart, on this last $3,500 of income she would be taxed at 43% instead of 27%.

Evelyn decided to make an RRSP contribution for $4,000 but only take the tax deduction for $3,500. (We all have the ability to make a contribution but delay taking the corresponding deduction.) This strategy accomplished several things. First, the RRSP deduction reduced her taxable income to $29,500 and eliminated the need for her to pay the more expensive tax that year at the 43% level. Second, by making an RRSP contribution she got an immediate tax deduction that year, reducing her tax bill and improving her cash flow. Third, she tax-sheltered as much investable wealth as she could, growing her RRSP and deferring tax on investment income until a future withdrawal from her RRSP. Fourth, she carried forward $500 of unused deduction to next year in order to apply it against *higher-tax-rate income* and get more tax refund for her RRSP dollars. Evelyn can continue to selectively apply her RRSP deductions when she chooses in order to minimize paying tax at the higher tax brackets.

Delaying taking a deduction this year can be a good strategy if the tax benefit outweighs the opportunity cost given up by not taking the deduction this year to get a larger tax refund now. For Evelyn, knowing her marginal tax rate permits her to "fine-tune" her RRSP strategies to maximize her deduction value — and minimize tax paid.

▼

Bonus Tip

Determining your spouse's marginal tax rate will help to determine who should save and who should pay expenses in the family. The lower earner should be the one saving (outside of RRSPs), since less tax will be payable if the lower earner is generating investment income than if the higher earner is saving and paying tax on the income.

STRATEGY #2

Avoid Year-End Mutual Fund Purchases

All year long, *mutual funds* may provide *unit holders* with investment income. They may also increase in value as the fund investments appreciate. This appreciation will provide unit holders with a capital gain on the eventual sale of the fund units. Both the income and the appreciation of investments accumulate inside the fund, and they are reflected through an increasing fund price.

Monthly, quarterly, or at year end, funds may make *distributions* (of the income or gains earned inside the fund) to the unit holders. The nature of a mutual fund trust is such that certain types of income earned by the investments owned by the trust — dividends or capital gains — retain their identity when distributed to individuals. These distributions reduce the value of fund units by the amount of the distributions per unit. Unit holders receiving distributions will have to pay tax on the distributions if the mutual fund is owned outside an RRSP.

Because of the year-end process described above, if you purchase mutual funds late in the year you may pay an increased fund price (reflecting the accumulated income inside the fund), and then witness a reduction of this price on (perhaps) December 31, when a distribution is paid to you as a unit holder. This can also occur quarterly if distributions are made quarterly, semi-annually, or monthly.

As a new fund buyer, you have paid for the income and gains that may have accrued inside the fund all year long, even though you didn't earn them. The result is that you are prepaying tax on future increases in value. These distributions will be taxed at your marginal tax rate if this investment is held outside an RRSP or RRIF.

Worse still, someone who purchases the same fund early in the following year (after distributions are made), at a reduced price (because of the distributions), doesn't have to pay any tax because he or she didn't receive any distributions from the previous year. He or she is currently ahead of you by the amount of tax you will have to pay in April, simply because of the timing of the purchase.

You could have avoided this tax pitfall by waiting until after the distribution was made to make your purchase — on January 1 or later of the next year. But bear in mind that some will argue that waiting until the next year may cost you more in lost return than you will save in tax. This may occur, so you need to balance the risk of lost return with the disadvantage of paying additional tax.

▼

Example

Tom purchased 100 units of XY mutual fund late in December 1996 for $5,000 or $50 per unit. On December 31, 1996, XY mutual fund paid Tom a distribution of $5 per unit, which was reinvested in the fund to buy approximately 11 more units ($500 of income/$45; when Tom was paid this distribution by the fund, the fund unit market price dropped to $45 per unit). The distribution was regular income, according to the T3 slip Tom received early in the new year from the fund company.

Tom had to pay 50% tax on the $500 of distributions, since he was in the top marginal tax bracket in his province. In total, Tom now had 111 units worth $5,000; the same value as before, but he also had to pay tax of 50% x $500 on distributions, or $250. His investment was worth $5,000, but cost him $5,250.

Sharon, Tom's wife, made exactly the same purchase only days later, in January 1997. She paid $45 per unit for 111 units, for a total of approximately $5,000. But she had no additional tax to pay, because she was receiving no income from the funds for the previous year. Sharon was ahead of Tom by $250 strictly because of the timing of the purchase.

So consider waiting until the new year when buying those year-end bargains! They may not be the bargains you think they are.

STRATEGY #3

Invest in Growth Investments Outside Your RRSP

The growth investments we are talking about here are *equity mutual funds.* These funds generally invest in *common shares* of *public corporations.* An equity mutual fund might, for example, own stock of the XYZ Bank of Canada. This stock may regularly pay dividends to the fund which are then distributed to you as the unit holder. Additionally, when the *fund manager* sells the stock inside the fund and buys stock of another corporation, there may be a capital gain on the sale of the shares. Again, this capital gain is distributed to you.

Many equity mutual funds distribute at least some dividends, capital gains, and even interest income annually. If you hold these investments outside your RRSP, you pay tax on these distributions, even if the funds are automatically reinvested in more fund units. This may not be a desirable scenario — paying tax on income and gains you don't even get (because it is reinvested). This income is reported on those *T3 slips* you get at tax time every spring.

However, some mutual funds are more "*tax smart.*" These are mutual funds that do not make significant *distributions* to investors each year. How do they do this? By purchasing investments in companies focused on growth of their business rather than on generating income to shareholders through dividend payments — *stocks* with increasing *share* price, resulting in part from reinvestment of earnings they might otherwise have paid out as dividends to shareholders. These companies use the money to grow, hire employees, upgrade systems, etc. A mutual fund holding such "growth" companies should not generate much regular income since the fund investments are not generating any. Instead, your return is composed of increasing value of the stocks owned by the fund, a value that isn't taxable until the stock is disposed of by the fund manager or you sell your fund units. In other words, taxation of your return is deferred!

Fund managers can also minimize taxable distributions by selling investments inside the mutual fund less frequently. (See Strategy #14 on the benefits of a buy-and-hold strategy.) Sales trigger the realization of any accrued capital gains that might exist on a stock investment made by the fund. Holding on to the stock longer defers the *realization of the gain* that would be allocated to you as a unit holder, and thus you can also defer the payment of tax.

Be on the lookout for fund managers who trade heavily and/or hold large *cash positions.* Heavy trading may generate large amounts of *taxable capital gains,* which are distributed to you and you will be taxed on. Cash levels inside a fund may produce interest income that is taxable to you at the highest rates applicable to investment income. Note that fund managers may not pay much attention to tax-smart investing since showing the highest *pre-tax return* is generally what they are ranked and rewarded on.

Overall, if you can find a fund that doesn't buy and sell heavily each year and also invests in stocks paying little or no distributions, you may be able to create an RRSP effect outside of your RRSP but without the *tax deduction.* Without selling investments or receiving income from those investments, you may be able to earn pure *tax-deferred growth* from the rising value of the mutual fund. As we learned earlier, accruing capital gains are not taxed until the related investment is disposed of. However, be cautious in selecting these investments. Remember, as a mutual fund unit holder, you cannot control when the fund manager sells the investments the fund owns.

▼

Example

Heather has been renting her home for a long time, and is interested in purchasing some equity mutual funds for saving purposes in order to buy a condominium for retirement in eight years' time. She had her investment advisor provide her with a list of three equity funds that had paid little or no distributions recently:

- ABC Canadian Equity Fund: good returns last three years; MER of 2.80%; distributed $0.10 in dividends, $0.10 of capital gains, and $0.05 of interest per unit to unit holders last year.
- DEF Canadian Growth Fund: good returns last three years; MER of 2.25%; no distributions last year.
- GHI Canadian Fund: good returns last three years; MER of 1.50%; distributed $0.30 in dividends per unit to unit holders last year.

Heather decided on the DEF mutual fund, because it has paid no distributions in the last three years and has seen a significant increase in unit value from appreciation in the share prices of the underlying investments. The fund manager's style is one of "value," meaning that he tries to buy stocks that are *undervalued* and then hold them for the long term for capital appreciation ("buy-and-hold" strategy). This means there shouldn't be much stock-selling each year by the fund manager. Owning this fund will allow Heather to accumulate savings through deferred growth on the fund, which will be taxable only when the fund is sold. Of course, there may be some taxable distributions, particularly when sales are required to fund large redemptions. But most distributions hopefully will be minimized through Heather's fund selection and understanding of fund management policies ("buy-hold" style).

Heather's investment advisor pointed out that the same strategy could be implemented in another way, with a bit more control for Heather. She could purchase a stock — not a fund — that doesn't pay any dividends, and hold the stock until a point in the future. Since she owns the stock directly, she controls all buy-and-sell decisions. No tax would result until the stock is sold and a capital gain is realized. (Unfortunately, the trade-off when buying stocks directly is that you may not have enough money to create a broadly diversified portfolio and will have higher investment risk as a result.)

The investment advisor also pointed out one other interesting point: sometimes a mutual fund appears to produce little or no distributions annually and therefore seems quite tax efficient. Upon closer examination of the fund, however, you may notice that the fund actually does earn dividend and interest income but this income is eaten up by management expenses charged against the fund by the *fund company*. When this happens, the income appears to disappear like it never existed, and there are no distributions. The investment advisor advised Heather not to be fooled by these types of funds where a high *management expense ratio* (MER) offsets the distributions, making it appear tax efficient. A lower MER and some distributions is usually better than high expenses where you get nothing at all. With some distributions, even after-tax, you are at least left with something in your pocket.

STRATEGY #4

Purchase Funds Holding Small Accrued Gains

This is a hard strategy to implement, because everyone wants to own successful mutual funds. Unfortunately, many of us tend to jump in after the fund has already been successful for a while. This is not always a smart move. Here's why. A successful *equity mutual fund* is one in which the *fund manager* purchased stocks that have since increased in value. This increase in stock value inside the fund means the value of the mutual fund has increased and the fund is holding several stock investments with accrued capital gains. Now you come along and want to buy the fund.

What happens when you buy a successful equity fund that is holding many stocks that have already increased in value? You are buying a fund that is holding accrued capital gains you didn't earn yet that you will be paying tax on. If the fund sells those stocks tomorrow, the tax liability arising from the sale of those stocks is distributed to you (and other unit holders) in the form of a taxable capital gain. At tax time, you will pay tax on gains you may not have earned but received as a distribution. Of course, this matters only for funds owned outside of an RRSP or RRIF. Also, this tax issue is more of a concern with funds that practise *buy-and-hold* policies than with funds that buy and sell often. Frequent selling of stocks may not allow time for large capital gains to accumulate in the fund, so you will be more likely to buy a fund with smaller accrued gains. The drawback is that the frequent selling by the fund manager does result in more frequent taxation of capital gains.

One way to minimize the chance of buying a fund with significant accrued tax liabilities is to purchase a brand-new mutual fund when it first becomes available. In this case, the mutual fund likely has just recently purchased many of the investments it holds, and accrued capital gains may be small.

Another option is to purchase equity funds inside your RRSP or RRIF, where taxation of income and capital gains is not an issue. This option, however, does not let you enjoy the *tax-advantaged* capital gains earned from stocks and equity funds held outside an RRSP or RRIF.

Tax-smart investing suggests that *equities* should be a part of many balanced RRSP/RRIF and non-RRSP/RRIF portfolios. Be aware of the existence of potential accrued tax liabilities when purchasing equity funds with large accrued capital gains buried in their portfolio. If you want to buy a "hot" fund, watch for funds that are "*capped*" or closed off to new investment, and then watch for the *fund company* to replicate the old fund — that is, create a similar fund. That may be a better time to buy: when the tax base on the investments is fresh and no significant capital gains yet exist.

Yet another way to avoid these hidden tax liabilities is to move out of mutual funds and pooled funds completely, and utilize *segregated money management* through a *money manager*, or through a segregated *wrapped product*. These products use your money to purchase a new portfolio of stocks and bonds such that the tax you pay on accrued capital gains is directly attributable to your market successes. For more information, see Strategy #25 on segregated wrapped products.

A final tip: where you do intend to buy the new similar fund, investigate just how similar it is. Mutual fund companies in Canada have produced some "*clone*" funds that have higher fees. If this is the case, you may want to compare the long-term profitability of the new fund with its small existing accrued capital gains versus a less expensive fund with larger accrued capital gains.

▼

Example

Peter just received $15,000 from the sale of stock he inherited 10 years ago when his cost base was only $1,000. He realizes that he will have to pay tax relating to the capital gain next year, so he has put $3,000 in a GIC to cover the expected tax bill (based on his calculation of tax using his *marginal tax rate*). The other $12,000 he wants to invest long-term outside his RRSP in a good-quality Canadian equity mutual fund.

After some research, Peter found what he thought was a superb mutual fund which had just produced a 40% return annually for the last two years. Newspapers reported that investors were contributing millions of dollars of new money to the fund each week. Peter decided this was the fund to buy, but he wanted a second opinion from his investment advisor.

After the advisor assessed Peter's objectives, needs, and *risk tolerance,* she confirmed that Peter's pick made sense. The advisor also told Peter to wait a month, because the fund was about to be "capped" or closed off to new investment due to its phenomenal growth. The advisor knew that the fund company was going to create a new fund which would be a clone of the first.

▼

Bonus Tip

For Peter and all investors, there can be significant tax advantages in buying the new clone fund instead of the old one. While the two funds contain similar investments, the tax impact on new investors may be quite different. In the old fund, investments that have done well over the last two years may have large accrued capital gains which will be distributed to fund unit holders when the stock is eventually sold inside the fund. As mentioned before, in this case a new investor may be allocated a large taxable gain that he or she hasn't earned but has inherited when the fund was bought, and will have to pay the related tax on. If the investor buys the new mutual fund instead, he or she can buy virtually the same investments but without the built-in tax liability. Since all the stock investments will be recent purchases in the new fund, new investors will be taxed on whatever gains they earn. However, the longer they wait to buy the new fund, the more likely they are to run into the same problem — so it is important to buy early.

STRATEGY #5

Don't Rush to Buy Mutual Funds on a Deferred-Load Basis

Did you know that when you bought your last mutual fund investment for your RRSP and chose the *deferred-load* fee option (deferred service charge) instead of paying a *front-end-load* fee, you may have chosen the more expensive fee option?

Mutual funds are often sold with no upfront fee to you but with a declining deferred-load fee which you will potentially never pay — if you hold the fund long enough. Inside your RRSP, where you are usually investing for 10 years or more, this sounds great. But it may not be. There is another set of expenses that all mutual fund owners pay annually. Inside the mutual fund the *fund company* charges the fund administrative expenses, operating expenses, and management fees to maintain the fund. These fees are deducted from the fund's annual gross return to produce the net rate of return you get. These internal fees are collectively called *management expenses*, and are expressed in the form of a *management expense ratio* (MER).

Understanding how these internal fees work is important,

because some fund companies offer two or more similar mutual funds with different fee options. In such cases, the internal fees can also vary widely from fund to fund. For example, if you buy X fund on a deferred-load basis, the internal management fees for this fund may be 2.50% each year. You may never know about the internal fees if you tend to focus on the net return to you after these fees are deducted; that's how the returns are shown in the newspapers. However, the fund company may also offer another fund (with similar investment holdings to those of X fund) that is being sold with a *front-end-load* fee of 2% but an internal fee of only 2.25%. While the idea of paying a 2% upfront fee may not appear attractive to you, and it's an easier sell for your investment advisor to sell you a fund with no upfront fee, over several years you may be earning less with the deferred-load fund, because of the reduced net return due to its higher *annual* internal fees.

To determine which is the least expensive alternative for you, ask your advisor (1) to tell you if the funds you are considering buying have multiple expense options for similar funds, and (2) to calculate which option is less costly to you depending on your needs. Evaluate these considerations alongside the advisor's first responsibility — to make you money!

▼

Example

Calvin had been relying on his mutual fund agent to sell him the right funds for his RRSP. He hadn't given much thought to the funds the agent recommended, but had assumed the agent had researched the picks and what he was buying was the best. That's why Calvin was surprised recently when he attended a *financial planning* meeting with an advisor, set up by Calvin's employer. When the advisor reviewed Calvin's mutual fund holdings, he told Calvin that with some of his mutual fund holdings, his agent had selected the more expensive fee option where there were similar funds.

Calvin had thought that by paying on a deferred-load basis he had chosen the cheaper way to buy. The advisor explained that buying on a deferred-load basis avoided only the purchase *commission* on the buying of a fund. But the funds in question had a higher internal expense ratio (MER) than the similar front-end-load funds offered by the same fund company. Depending how long Calvin plans on owning the funds, he may pay more through internal fund expenses than any load would ever cost.

Additionally, the advisor noted that one of the deferred-load funds that Calvin bought attributed much of its past success to a *star manager* who recently left the fund to join a competitor. The fund company had replaced the star with a relatively unproven manager. Since Calvin has been encouraged to hold long-term because he bought on a deferred-load basis, unless he sells and pays the deferred load, he doesn't get the benefit of a fund managed by the successful manager who had attracted him in the first place.

Calvin's advisor told him that before he purchases any funds he should inquire if the particular fund has a sister fund with a different fee structure. If there are sister funds with different MERs, he should consider having his advisor evaluate which will be the least expensive option during the planned holding period.

Crunching the Numbers

What Calvin bought: he paid $1,000 for a mutual fund with an internal MER of 2.25%. He bought on a deferred-load basis so there were no purchasing fees. Instead, the deferred load declined to zero after seven years.

At the end of 20 years, assuming an 8% growth rate less

the 2.25% MER, full reinvestment of income, and that these investments have been held inside an RRSP, the fund Calvin bought will be worth approximately $3,000.

What Calvin could have bought: he could have paid $1,000 for a sister fund that includes a 2% front-end-load fee. The fee will be $20, and the net investment amount will be $980. However, this fund has an internal MER of only 2.00%.

Under the same assumptions, the fund Calvin could have bought would be worth approximately $3,100 in 20 years. While the difference appears small here, keep in mind that on $100,000 (instead of $1,000), this difference is almost $10,000.

STRATEGY #6

Invest in Some Index Mutual Funds

Index mutual funds are investment products that attempt to mirror the *performance* of recognized capital market indices. These mutual funds may purchase the same stocks in the same proportions that exist inside a particular *index*, or they may purchase derivatives that lock in the change of an index (see Strategy #7). Indices like the *TSE 300* in Canada and the S&P 500 in the United States are examples of indices mutual funds have attempted to mirror. *Bond* market indices are also commonly replicated, primarily tracking the Scotia Capital Markets Universe Bond Index in Canada. Equity indices may consist of the largest companies in their respective countries. Some indices include companies that are representative of industries and the economy of the country in general. Other indices are more industry or country specific.

A mutual fund that attempts to mirror an index by purchasing similar stock and bond holdings tries to have similar performance as the index less a fee to the fund company to manage the fund and pay the operating costs. Performance may also differ slightly if the fund company doesn't buy and sell shares of stock at the same time the index changes the companies in the index, a difference generally referred to as *tracking error.* Generally, however, the performance of an index mutual fund should be very similar to the actual index, less fees.

For tax-smart investors, index funds can be attractive. There are several reasons to consider purchasing index funds:

- Index funds that mirror the TSE 300 or S&P 500 consist of investments that generally are the largest and some of the most successful companies in Canada and the U.S. respectively. Owning the investments included in these indices serves to diversify your money across industries and countries, and this reduces the risk of a significant loss occurring because of a loss in one particular region or industry sector.
- Indices like the TSE 300 traditionally have had low turnover of stocks in the index. This translates to an index fund that holds most of its portfolio year after year (a form of buy-and-hold), and deferral of taxation of gains. This differs from a fund that buys and sells frequently, potentially incurring *taxable capital gains* with each sale.
- Index funds are usually fully invested. This means that the funds have little or no cash balances earning a low rate of return. Also, the interest income generated by cash balances is *tax disadvantaged* because of the high tax rate applied to it. Index funds may have little or no interest income, depending on the nature of the funds, increasing the potential to earn *tax-advantaged* dividends and capital gains. In successful markets where stock prices are rising, holding cash can be a disadvantage, while in down markets holding cash can reduce losses.
- Over the long term, index funds outperform many actively managed funds in the U.S. and Canada. While many funds now and then will outperform an index fund, far

fewer can do it consistently over time. Ask your investment advisor to compare your Canadian equity funds to the TSE 300 over the last five years and see if the active management has outperformed a passively managed index with no manager.

- Index funds usually have lower MERs than their actively managed counterparts. Without salaries to pay for managers and no need to fly to (say) Brazil to research new investments, the cost of running the funds can be a lot less. Unfortunately, however, in many cases index funds are low cost because they pay no commissions or trailer fees to brokers or advisors and, sadly, may not be recommended to clients because of this.
- With index funds, understanding how well you are doing is easier. If you own an index fund that tracks the TSE 300, you can usually find the return for the TSE 300 in most Canadian newspapers, and this should approximate your fund's rate of return (less fees). If you own an actively managed fund, you have to search a little harder to find out how well you are doing.

▼

Example

Shannon usually picks current *hot funds* for her new RRSP investments. These are funds that everyone is buying, usually because of outstanding performance resulting from good active management. This year Shannon's investment advisor introduced her to index mutual funds and suggested she consider some of these funds for a piece of her investment portfolio. Shannon was initially sceptical — she is attracted by the potential of big returns — but the investment advisor demonstrated how many active funds in Canada do not beat the index funds, yet these active funds in some cases charge three times as much in MERs. Talk about paying more to underperform!

Shannon started to like the idea of owning some index mutual funds. She decided to invest in index funds because she liked the possibility of building a strong core of blue-chip index funds around which she could add active managers. She had her investment advisor set up a monthly transfer to an index fund that mirrored the TSE 300 for her Canadian content. She also had her advisor set up a monthly transfer to a U.S. equity mutual fund that mirrored the S&P 500. (The U.S. component was limited to her permissible 20% *foreign content* limit.)

Shannon is now committed to owning some index mutual funds. She knows that her index funds are invested in North America's biggest companies, which is less risky than the way her other funds are invested. She likes not having to worry about her favourite money manager leaving the current hot fund, since index funds have no managers. She likes that the fund management is minimal (because index funds are designed only to match the broadly recognized index) and therefore the fund company charges much lower fees compared to the fees of equity funds that require *active management.*

Shannon was also impressed with the long-term historical returns for her two index funds. In many cases they exceed the returns of many actively managed funds investing in Canada and the U.S. And when she factored in the loads of actively managed funds, their higher MERs, and the taxation that results when funds buy and sell frequently, index funds became even more attractive.

Shannon admits she still wants to buy some hot funds and some other actively managed funds that she thinks can beat the market indices routinely. However, she is committed to adding these types of funds as "flavour" around her core holding of index funds.

STRATEGY #7

Know When to Buy Natural Versus Synthetic Index Funds

I have already encouraged you to invest in *index mutual funds* (see Strategy #6). Now let's fine-tune that strategy. Buy *natural index funds* outside an RRSP and buy *synthetic index funds* inside an RRSP.

Natural index funds are funds that replicate an index by purchasing the underlying investments that compose the index. For a Canadian equity index fund, for example, the fund manager might purchase the stock of corporations included in the TSE 300 in the same proportion that they appear in the index. Synthetic index funds are funds that may use *derivatives* to purchase exposure to a particular index. Synthetic funds are more fully described in Strategy #44. A synthetic fund may use a *futures* contract to provide investors with a rate of return equal to the change in the index.

While these two types of index funds appear to be similar, they can be very different for tax purposes. Generally, distributions from synthetic index funds are taxed as ordinary income in Canada because they earn *interest income* from *Treasury bill* investments and ordinary income from derivatives. Some index fund managers have concluded that the distributions from the derivatives are more appropriately treated as capital gains. Keep in mind, however, that if you take this position in your tax return (treating the distributions as capital gains), you may be challenged by Revenue Canada.

Since natural index funds hold investments in real companies, they are *tax advantaged* compared to synthetic funds holding derivatives. Natural funds can flow out to unit holders the dividends paid by the funds' corporate investments. They can also flow out capital gains earned on the sale of their stock when the index changes. These dividends and capital gains are tax advantaged in Canada.

What does this all mean? It means that *tax-smart* investing indicates you should invest in natural index funds outside your RRSP or RRIF, where tax effectiveness matters, and invest in synthetic index funds inside your RRSP or RRIF, where tax is less important.

How can you tell whether an index fund is synthetic or not? Look at the fund holdings as provided by your investment advisor. If the holdings consist of shares in companies, you have found a natural index fund. If the holdings are Treasury bills and some futures contracts, you have likely found a synthetic index fund. Alternatively, ask your investment advisor to determine which funds are natural and which are synthetic.

▼

Example

Lana is a believer in index fund investing and already holds some global index funds inside her RRSP. She recently received a cash gift from her grandmother and decided to invest this money as a long-term investment outside her RRSP. She wanted to investigate more equity index funds, so she turned to her financial advisor for help. Because the financial advisor had sold Lana her other index funds, she knew Lana was already knowledgeable about the characteristics of the investment. But because the previous purchase was inside the RRSP, the advisor hadn't explained the tax effects of different types of index funds. Now appeared to be the right time.

Lana is currently in the highest tax bracket in Canada and is taxed at approximately 50% on all new *regular income.* Another index fund investment would provide new income, so the financial advisor explained to Lana how she should strive to obtain some dividends from her index funds in order to obtain favourable tax treatment. The advisor explained how synthetic index funds may distribute only regular income, which would be taxed at a higher rate than dividends or capital gains. A similar investment, but the potential for a much different after-tax return!

Crunching the Numbers

Calculating After-Tax Return on Two Index Funds

XYZ Synthetic Fund: $1,000 invested on January 1, 1996, earned 10% ($100) during 1996. The fund was sold on January 1, 1997. The investment return was taxed as regular income, thus the $100 earnings were taxed at Lana's marginal tax rate of 50% for regular income.

QRS Natural Fund: $1,000 invested for the same time period, earning the same rate of return, and sold on the same date. The investment return consisted of 3% dividends and 7% capital gain on the sale. The returns were taxed at Lana's marginal tax rate of 34% for dividends and 38% for capital gains.

The synthetic fund produced an after-tax return of $50. The natural fund produced an after-tax return of $63.20. Lana was surprised at the difference in the tax impact between the two similar funds. Without the advisor's counsel, she wouldn't have known the difference.

STRATEGY #8

Invest in Mutual Fund Corporations

A great advantage of an *RRSP* or *RRIF* is the tax-deferred compounding of income that occurs over time. Some mutual funds structured as corporations also give you some tax-deferred compounding — much like your RRSP or RRIF does — but in this case the *deferral of tax* is available outside an RRSP.

Some mutual fund companies offer mutual funds structured through a *mutual fund corporation* rather than a traditional mutual fund trust. The corporation issues several classes of *shares*, with each share class investing in a different underlying mutual fund. You as an investor are permitted to switch among the share classes — this is similar to switching among different funds — without triggering a *capital gain.* As long as your investment remains within the corporate structure, any capital gains are deferred. If you redeem fund shares, however, this will trigger taxation on all gains and losses that have occurred.

One of the key advantages of these mutual fund corporations is the tax deferral on capital gains that is available to an investor who wants to actively manage his or her investment portfolio by switching among the different share classes. Note, however, that although the switching between classes is tax free, there may be tax consequences for the investor anyway. If the fund corporation has to sell stocks attributable to an existing share class in order to provide funds for the switch, taxable gains may find their way to the investors. This will ultimately depend on several factors, including the level of redemptions, capital gains and losses attributable to other share classes, and fund expenses.

▼

Example

Anna owns several *equity mutual funds* outside her RRSP. She likes to jump around between funds as she tries to time purchases and sales to take advantage of optimal performance, but for tax purposes she has been incurring capital gains each time she sells a fund (she is a successful investor!). She doesn't enjoy the tax she has been paying on these capital gains, so last year she looked into mutual fund corporations as an alternative.

Anna used cash from some matured *GICs* to purchase a balanced portfolio of mutual funds through a fund corporation structure. This year, when Anna prepared her tax return, she was pleased by the reduction in tax liability. The reduction was due to the elimination of some interest income from the GICs, and the fact that her mutual funds owned through the corporate structure were sheltering capital gains from tax she attracted each time she switched between funds.

Sure, tax will have to be paid on the eventual redemption of the investments, but in the meantime, a tax deferral is welcomed by Anna.

Crunching the Numbers

Anna's old equity funds: Anna sold Equity Fund #1 to buy Equity Fund #2. A small gain was realized on the sale. Soon after, Equity Fund #2 was sold to buy Equity Fund #3. A large gain was realized on Equity Fund #2. This all happened in one month as Anna continued to make money in the market. It appears she is succeeding, as she made $2,000 in capital gains and $300 of dividends from her trading and her holdings.

Anna's new equity funds: In the same month, Anna flipped between three equity funds within the mutual fund corporation. She had similar success, again making $2,000 in capital gains and $300 of dividends.

While there appears to be no difference in profitability, when it is time to pay tax on Anna's successful investing, the $2,000 in capital gains earned inside the mutual fund corporation will not be taxed yet. These gains will be tax deferred until Anna eventually sells out of the new funds and the mutual fund corporation completely. The regular equity fund gains will cause $760 of tax to be paid next year, while none will be due on the new funds. A big difference!

An Important Reminder

The mutual fund corporation structure that Anna invested in can defer the taxation of gains earned on the difference between the cost and proceeds of the fund invested in, as described above. But as also noted, the *distributions* of capital gains, dividends, and interest earned inside the fund are not tax sheltered (similar to mutual fund trusts) and can find their way to the investor, who will have to pay tax on these distributions as received.

STRATEGY #9

Keep Proper Mutual Fund Records to Minimize Tax

Outside Your RRSP

Keeping track of the correct cost of your mutual funds is important because it can reduce the amount of tax you pay. This record-keeping can be confusing however, especially if you are trading frequently.

Owners of mutual funds held outside their *RRSP* will receive *T3 slips* each spring reporting all *interest, dividends, foreign income* (and non-business tax paid), and *capital gains* distributions from the previous year. Whether you received these *distributions* or had them reinvested automatically, they are included in your income and therefore are taxable.

When the income and capital gains are reinvested to purchase additional units, the total distribution amount is added to the original cost of the mutual fund investment in order to calculate the new cost base. Therefore, the cost base of your investment will consist of your original purchase cost plus any distributions that have been reinvested. Failure to remember to add these taxed distributions to your cost base will result in double taxation of your earnings, since a larger capital gain (due to the understated cost base) will result when the investment is eventually sold.

Inside Your RRSP

It is a good idea to maximize the *foreign content* inside your RRSP since global investment *diversification* can serve to reduce your overall *investment risk*. RRSP foreign content limits are based on the cost of investments inside the RRSP: only 20% of the cost of all investments can be foreign property.

It is therefore in your best interest to increase the Canadian investment cost base in order to maximize the permissible foreign content. This can be accomplished by regularly selling and repurchasing Canadian equity investments that have increased in value inside your RRSP and reinvesting foreign equity distributions in Canadian investments, since the gains (both Canadian and foreign) will be added to the cost base of Canadian investments and total investments. This will permit you to purchase additional foreign investments in your RRSP. Watch those transaction fees, though!

Finally, here is a word of caution about account transfers. If you have recently transferred an RRSP account *in kind* from one institution to another, I suggest you go back and ensure that the receiving institution picked up the correct cost bases to calculate the foreign content limit. The new institution may have incorrectly used the fair market value of investments at the time of transfer, rather than the purchase costs, as the new base to calculate the foreign content limit. This can lead to an overstatement or understatement of your permissible foreign content limit depending on your particular situation. An overstatement of the limit could result in penalties from Revenue Canada, while an understatement could unnecessarily reduce your ability to invest outside of Canada.

▼

Example

Meghan owned an equity mutual fund which her parents had purchased for her 10 years ago as an education fund. They had invested the proceeds of a gift Meghan had received from non-resident grandparents, and all the fund's income was reinvested in additional fund units. In each of those 10 years, Meghan received a T3 slip for dividends earned on the fund and included this dividend income on her tax return.

Six months ago, at age 24, Meghan sold the equity fund in order to use the proceeds to fund her education. Now it's time to do her personal tax return and she has been wondering what the tax implications of the sale are. She visited her father's tax accountant for advice. The tax accountant informed Meghan that she would have to pay tax on a capital gain resulting from the sale, since the fund had significantly appreciated in value. The amount of the capital gain would be the proceeds from the sale less the cost base less any transaction fees. The cost base consisted of the original cost of all fund purchases, plus any distributions received that had been reinvested.

Together, Meghan and the tax accountant reviewed Meghan's income from the mutual fund over the last 10 years. They added up the income from the fund and all of the new purchases to produce a total. The tax accountant told Meghan that this total is the adjusted cost base, which is used on her tax return for this year. She should deduct this cost base from the sale proceeds to calculate the capital gain. She should also remember to deduct any load fees and other transaction costs she may have incurred to buy or sell the fund. She should then multiply the remaining capital gain by 75% to produce the taxable capital gain that is reported on page one of the jacket of her tax return and included in her *taxable income.* (Revenue Canada only taxes three-quarters of a capital gain.)

Meghan found the experience with the accountant to be a lesson for the future. She learned that whenever she buys mutual funds outside an RRSP, the accounting for the funds can be confusing and time consuming. Additional purchases and switching between funds can make it even more complicated. However, keeping track of the correct mutual fund costs is important in order to ensure that no additional tax is paid on the eventual sale of the funds.

Crunching the Numbers

The tax accountant and Meghan calculated her cost base and the capital gain of the fund she sold, as follows:

Original purchase amount, 10 years ago: **$10,000**

Annual distributions of dividends (taxed in the year received, and reinvested when received):

Year	Distribution ($)
1	500
2	505
3	515
4	508
5	0
6	460
7	550
8	555
9	555
10	0

(the fund was sold early in year ten)

Total cost base (original price plus tax-paid distributions): $14,148

Proceeds on sale: $16,000

Broker's fees incurred to sell: $160

Capital gain: ($16,000 – $14,148) – $160 = $1,692

Taxable capital gain: **$1,692 x 75% = $1,269**

STRATEGY #10

Think Tax Before Selling Your Non-RRSP Mutual Funds

Remember when you filed your 1994 tax return and you *crystallized* accrued gains on your *non-RRSP* mutual funds as of February 22, 1994? That crystallization produced an *exempt capital gains balance* for each fund, representing an account against which you can offset future *taxable capital gains* produced from that same mutual fund. That credit exists to help you to reduce future income tax incurred on capital gains either allocated from the fund or realized from the redemption of fund units.

You can utilize the account in two ways. One way is to use the account balance to offset any capital gains *distributions* made by the same mutual fund. An account balance can only be applied against distributions from that same fund elected on in 1994. The second way to use the account balance is when you actually sell fund units and realize a capital gain on the sale. The account balance can be used to offset the capital gain realized on the sale.

All of this means that you have the ability to earn tax-free capital gains generated by a mutual fund until the exempt gains balance is nil. If all the remaining units of a fund on which you claimed the capital gains exemption are sold and an exempt gains balance remains after the final sale, the remainder is added to the cost base immediately prior to the fund sale, producing a capital loss which can be used to offset other capital gains.

When you are determining which funds to sell, one of the things to look at is whether a related exempt gains balance exists. The existence of this account increases your after-tax return on the funds, so in some cases it may make sense to sell these funds before you sell others that have no exempt gains balance.

But remember, tax is only one of the factors to consider in deciding to sell investments. If you expect good performance in the future, a current sale (albeit tax free) means you may forfeit possible future returns, which could offset the immediate tax savings.

▼

Example

Tracy had decided to take a three-month vacation to the Far East, and was deciding how she would pay for the trip. She had a collection of equity mutual funds which she had saved over the last five years, and decided she would sell a portion of these funds to pay for the vacation. Tracy contacted her investment advisor and asked him to sell some of the funds to produce cash of $5,000. She didn't care which funds he sold, and thought he should know what was best. He said he would review her portfolio for funds that made sense to sell, and they agreed on a meeting date to conclude on what to sell.

That night, Tracy was having dinner with her parents and told them she was looking forward to her trip. Her father, a partner with a local chartered accounting firm who was also Tracy's accountant, asked how she was going to pay for the vacation and offered to help her with a loan until she returned. Tracy said thanks but explained that she was selling some of the mutual funds she had accumulated over time. Her father, knowing the tax treatment he had given Tracy's mutual funds in her tax returns over the years, suggested that he review her mutual funds from a tax point of view to determine which would be the best to sell. He said he would do this before her meeting with the investment advisor. Tracy admitted that she had not thought about the tax side of selling.

The next day, Tracy's father stated that several of her funds had been crystallized in 1994 and had large exempt capital gains balances. The sale of these funds would reduce her tax liability, leaving her with more money in pocket for her trip.

Armed with this information, Tracy visited her investment advisor to determine which funds to sell. In the end, they were able to sell some of the funds that had exempt capital gains balances (funds that were sensible to sell now in any case). In a few cases, the exempt gains balances reduced her capital gains significantly, and in one case, a capital loss arose (because the exempt gains balance had a remainder) which offset more of the capital gains.

Because of the tax reductions, Tracy didn't have to sell as much of her investments as originally anticipated to produce the $5,000 she needed for her vacation.

Crunching the Numbers

Tracy's portfolio that was sold:

Fund	Proceeds	Cost Base	Exempt Gains Balance	Capital Gain
AXL Equity Fund	$2,600	$1,000	$1,000	$600
BMC Equity Fund	$2,000	$1,000	$200	$800
XJF Equity Fund	$1,200	$1,100	$1,500	($1,400)

Selling this portfolio will generate proceeds of $5,800 and no taxation since the capital loss that results from the remainder of the exempt gains balance for XJF Fund offsets all other capital gains that are taxable.

STRATEGY #11

Should You Buy Bond Mutual Funds or Bonds?

Should you own fixed income mutual funds ("*bond funds*") or should you purchase bonds directly? Did you know that many of the bond investments bond mutual funds own (e.g., Government of Canada bonds) can be purchased by you directly?

Bonds themselves are fixed income investments where the bond issuer is borrowing money from investors for a period of time and paying interest to the bond holder for use of the money. Bonds are rated for risk level and some can be actively traded in the marketplace. Market-traded bonds (Canada Savings Bonds are not market traded) vary in price according to changes in market interest rates. Depending on the change in rates, you have the potential to earn capital gains or losses if you sell a bond before it matures. If the bond matures at *face value*, you simply earn the interest promised on the bond.

Bond mutual funds are mutual funds that invest primarily in different types of bonds and other fixed income investments. Generally, a bond manager's role is to purchase new bonds as old ones mature, and to buy and sell bonds actively in the marketplace in an attempt to generate capital gains in addition to the bond interest income. Bond funds generally produce interest income and with some capital gains (or losses) potential depending on the bond fund manager's ability to buy and sell effectively.

Here are some pros and cons of owning bonds and bond funds:

- If a bond fund is owned outside an RRSP, active bond trading by the fund manager can produce *tax-advantaged* capital gains besides the regular bond fund interest income. (You can also earn capital gains when you own bonds directly, if you sell them before they mature and conditions are favourable.)
- Because someone else (the bond fund manager) is managing the buying and selling of investments, purchasing a bond fund can mean less investment management and may be attractive to less sophisticated investors.
- Bond funds may have enough money to enable them to purchase a diverse collection of bonds and fixed income investments. As with equity funds, *diversification* can help to reduce risk in some cases. Outside a bond fund, an investor may not have enough money to purchase a diversified portfolio of bonds since minimum investment amounts may be $5,000 or more for each bond.
- Because a bond fund can be actively managed by a bond manager, the potential exists for higher returns (interest plus capital gains). Individual investors owning bonds directly may be hard pressed to commit the time and expertise to replicate the bond fund manager's commitment to making investors more money.
- Bond funds may allow you to access specialty investments such as global bonds, higher-yielding bonds, and *emerging market bonds.* Access to these bonds by you directly

may be limited due to their steep minimum investment amounts.

- Bond funds, because of their size and financial clout, may be able to purchase large amounts of bonds at a lower cost than would be charged to an individual investor buying just one bond. This cost savings may be passed on to the investor through the bond fund's returns.
- Bond funds can be expensive for investors capable of managing their own portfolio of bonds. Bond fund *MERs* average more than 1.50% annually — plus any loads paid to purchase or sell the funds.
- Owners of bond funds may not be aware of the risk associated with the bond investments held by the funds. Bond fund managers may add higher-risk corporate bonds or royalty trusts to their portfolios without the investors knowing — possibly resulting in higher-risk bond portfolios than is desired. Owning bonds directly lets you more directly control the quality of the bonds you own by evaluating their creditworthiness and other characteristics of the issuers.
- Owning bonds directly allows investors to buy now and lock in a *yield* (the rate of return on the bond) until the bond matures. In other words, you know exactly what you'll have at the end of the period. With a bond fund, someone else manages the bond portfolio and you have no control over rate of return or when the manager buys and sells.
- Bond funds are easier and less expensive to purchase than bonds. Bond funds can be purchased for as little as a few hundred dollars, while market-traded bonds may cost several thousand dollars each.

So what is right for you, bonds or bond funds? It depends on what you are comfortable with, based on all the characteristics of both, how much money you have, your *risk tolerance,* and your need for *liquidity*, among other factors. Owning bonds directly gives you better direct control over your investment; you control the quality, the rate of return, and the maturity date.

Generally, investors with small amounts to invest and long time horizons may want to consider bond funds, since these give wide diversification of investments for limited amounts of money. A longer-term investor may more easily tolerate ups and downs of a bond fund managed by someone else striving to get higher returns. And generally, investors with more money and a shorter time period to invest may want to consider owning bonds directly if they want to lock in their rate of return and know how much money they will have on a certain date.

▼

Example

Jack is 65 and has just retired. He has started looking at his retirement portfolio recently and is trying to structure his retirement-income cash flow. Aside from his RRSP, Jack holds a large amount of GICs which are maturing soon. He doesn't plan on using his RRSP proceeds for several years and is happy with its current investment content.

Jack has heard about bonds and bond mutual funds and would like to utilize these investments to replace at least part of his GIC portfolio. He met with his investment advisor and they discussed the pros and cons of all of these fixed income investments, reviewed Jack's risk preferences, examined his overall asset mix, and determined his goals and cash needs. They developed an investment strategy that pleased Jack. Jack's strategy is outlined as follows:

- 20% of Jack's GIC portfolio will remain in GICs because he is used to GICs and isn't comfortable giving them up completely for something new. These GICs and the bonds described below will serve Jack's short-term (less than three years) cash needs.
- 50% of the GIC portfolio will be converted into five Government of Canada bonds of equal amounts, maturing each year for the next five years. The laddered strategy appeals to Jack because he wants to plan his cash flows for the next few years and having the fixed amounts mature one a year will provide an exact amount to be available to him each year.
- 30% of the GIC portfolio will be converted to a bond mutual fund holding high-quality bond investments. The bond fund is viewed by Jack as a five- to ten-year investment, where Jack is prepared to take a bit more risk by using an active bond manager in the hope of obtaining enhanced returns over that period of time. It's capital that Jack doesn't need to spend, and he can tolerate some ups and downs in that time period.

STRATEGY #12

Acquire Short-Term Investments to Mature After December 31

This is an easy way to defer paying tax on an investment for an entire year. If you are purchasing *bonds* or *GICs* outside an RRSP or RRIF and the maturity date will fall late in the year, pick investments that last a few days or months longer and will mature in the new year. Interest income is generally taxable annually and on maturity of the investment, under the *Income Tax Act of Canada.* The last interest payment will fall on maturity of the investment. By having the maturity fall at the beginning of the next year, you can defer paying tax on the income until the following tax season — another year away.

The same rule applies for stock investments. Rather than sell a stock in December and face taxation immediately on any *capital gains* realized, wait until January to sell the stock and defer paying tax on the gain for a whole year.

Obviously, these strategies must accommodate your need for the money and should be balanced with sound investment decisions. If, for example, you must sell late in the year because you need cash, the tax impact may become less important.

▼

Example

Susan owns several GICs in her *non-registered investment* portfolio. She has been in the habit of renewing one of these GICs every three months. Susan is waiting for interest rates to rise before she will buy a longer-term GIC. Meanwhile, she regularly receives an interest cheque from her financial institution for the earnings from the GICs, and she unhappily pays the income tax on these earnings.

It's now September, and Susan uses some new tax-smart investing knowledge and decides to purchase a four-month GIC instead of a three-month one on September 15 of the current year. The three-month GIC would have matured on December 15 of the current year and resulted in tax due on the income, but the new four-month GIC will mature in January, effectively deferring taxation of income earned on the four-month GIC for an entire year.

Deferring taxation of the GIC interest to the next year permits Susan to hold on to her money for the tax payment for an extra year, just by extending the maturity date by a month. Susan's GIC is large, and the tax deferral will be significant to her. Paying tax later means she will be able to invest the investment income for a longer time before having to pay tax on the income. This will generate even more income, which wouldn't have been possible if the income was needed this year to pay the tax bill.

STRATEGY #13

Invest Carefully Outside of Canada

I am one of the first people to sing the praises of investing outside of Canada. Not because Canada is a bad place to invest, but because Canada *could* be a bad place to invest, every once in a while. Global *diversification* can help to minimize the potential loss to your *portfolio* when a particular country is experiencing an economic downturn and poor economic performance. If Canada has a bad year, and you have invested in Canada, France, the United States, England, Australia, and Japan, then perhaps some of the other countries are having a good year which will offset your Canadian losses. If you have invested only in Canada, however, you don't even have this chance.

There are tax disadvantages to investing outside of Canada, though, and they relate to *dividends* in particular. Dividends received from Canadian *corporations* are one of the lowest-taxed types of investment income in Canada, and dividend-producing investments can play a role in many investors' portfolios. However, dividends received from non-Canadian corporations are not subject to the same tax-advantaged treatment as Canadian-source dividends. Instead, these foreign dividends are taxed as *regular income* — a big difference! That means you must purchase qualifying Canadian investments in order to take advantage of the preferential tax treatment available in Canada on dividend income. Whether they are from direct ownership in foreign stocks or ownership in international dividend funds, dividends are taxed as regular income if they are being received directly from non-Canadian companies.

Bearing this in mind, outside your RRSP and RRIF you should balance your global investing with some Canadian equity investments that pay Canadian dividends. This will ensure that you get some favourable tax treatment from earning Canadian dividends and reduce your tax bill on investment income.

An additional tip: some companies in Canada offer dividend-paying preferred shares denominated in foreign currencies (like U.S. dollars). This type of investment may permit you to access the lower taxation of Canadian-source dividends and still achieve global diversification by purchasing a foreign-currency investment. Diversification of investments across markets, currencies, and investment types can reduce your *investment risk*.

▼

Example

Barbara knew that dividend income is taxed in a preferential manner in Canada and she wanted to take advantage of this. Inside her RRSP she was holding several *international equity mutual funds*, which were generating dividends that were being categorized as *foreign income* for tax purposes. Barbara smiled because she knew that inside her RRSP, where taxation of investment income didn't matter, this income tax treatment on foreign investments had no impact. She wasn't being *tax disadvantaged*, and she was maximizing her *foreign content* through ownership of international investments.

However, outside of her RRSP she had bought a few units of the same fund. Barbara knew that while she was getting international exposure, she was losing the war on tax, since the foreign dividends were not being taxed at the lower rate applicable to Canadian dividends. Instead, the foreign dividends were been classified as foreign income as noted on her mutual fund T3 income slip last year.

With help from her advisor, Barbara decided not to sell these non-RRSP investments, because while they had appreciated nicely, the amount was small and to sell them would attract tax and additional transactions fees that would take several years to recover through tax savings from new Canadian investments generating Canadian dividends.

Instead, in the future Barbara would try to be more aware of the source of dividend-producing investments, and she would select some Canadian dividend-generating investments to take advantage of the favourable tax rates applicable to these dividends. International diversification would continue to be addressed through her RRSP and with some of her non-RRSP investments.

Crunching the Numbers

Barbara's current fund investment:

LOQ International Equity Fund generated the following income and gains last year:

Interest	$300
Capital gains	$250
Foreign income	$1,250

Total tax paid by Barbara (highest marginal rate):

$300 x 50%	
$250 x 38%	
$1,250 x 50%	**Total tax bill $870**

If Barbara was to convert the foreign income to Canadian dividend income by investing in a different equity fund, her tax savings could be $1,250 x (50% – 34%) = $200 every year.

STRATEGY #14

Utilize a Buy-and-Hold Investment Strategy to Delay Paying Tax

This strategy is all about controlling *asset turnover* on equity investments. The easiest way to avoid paying taxes in the short term is to delay the sale of any investments with *accrued capital gains* and to buy *equity mutual funds* that don't frequently sell the investments held inside those funds. As long as investments such as stocks or equity mutual funds are not sold by you, and the *fund managers* running the funds also *buy and hold* for longer periods of time, your investments can continue to appreciate in value without attracting immediate tax on the accruing capital gains. There will be tax to pay on any dividends distributed to you, but there is no taxation on capital gains until a *disposition* occurs. It's a simple "buy-and-hold" strategy.

This type of strategy may not be desirable with non-RRSP money where the funds are being saved for a specific short-term purpose and the intent is to dispose of the investments shortly. And bear in mind that this strategy is only a *deferral of tax*. Someday there will be a disposition or *deemed disposition* of this investment, when tax will be due on the capital gain realized. But in the meantime, next to a *tax deduction*, a tax deferral is the next best thing for the average Canadian trying to keep his or her tax bill low. Of course, it is an added benefit if you are in a lower tax bracket when you eventually sell the investments with the accrued gains (perhaps in retirement) and pay less tax overall on the investments than you might today.

This buy-and-hold strategy may work better for individual stocks than for mutual funds. Actively trading mutual fund managers will generate distributions of interest, dividends, and capital gains that are taxable. As an owner of an actively traded fund, you have no control over the generation of capital gains from the manager's buying and selling. All you can do is purchase funds that have a value-focused investing policy — that is, the manager's policy is to buy and hold. This type of fund will have reduced asset turnover, resulting in more deferred capital gains. You will continue to receive dividends and interest, though, since this type of income is not affected by turnover.

So when holding investments that appreciate in value, and where those increases will be taxed as capital gains, consider keeping the investments for longer periods. If you delay paying the tax on the capital gains, your investment capital is maximized and working for you. In terms of growing your *net worth*, the longer you can practise this strategy, the more net worth you should have over time, even after the tax is eventually paid.

▼

Example

Donna purchased 100 *shares* of the *common stock* of XYZ Bank as a long-term investment to add to her existing portfolio of GICs. Donna plans to sell both investments in the next eight years and use the proceeds to purchase a cottage.

A year after the stock purchase, Donna decided to purchase a new car and wanted to pay for the car using some of her invested funds. Since the stock purchase last year, the bank stock had appreciated nicely and was paying regular dividends to Donna as well. Using a tax-smart investing strategy, Donna waited for the GICs to mature and used the proceeds to purchase the vehicle. The GICs attracted no taxation other than the tax on the interest income she received.

By using the GIC proceeds instead of selling the bank stock to fund her cash need, Donna actually followed two tax-smart investing strategies: first, she avoided realizing a capital gain from the bank shares and paying the related tax; and second, she sold the investment that was producing the *higher-tax-rate income* — interest income is taxed at higher marginal tax rates than dividends. Rather than rushing out and selling any old investment to buy the car, Donna had thought about the tax consequences and minimized her tax bill this year.

Crunching the Numbers

Donna's successful buy-and-hold strategy

1,000 shares at $100/share, for a total cost of $100,000. Assuming a 12% growth rate annually, compounded, and excluding the impact of the dividends, this investment will be worth close to $248,000 at the end of eight years. At a tax rate of 38% for capital gains, Donna will pay $56,240 in tax — ($248K – $100K) x 38%. This will leave her with after-tax cash of $191,760 for the cottage.

Had Donna bought and sold more frequently

Now suppose Donna had made the same investments under the same conditions, but sold the shares at the end of the fourth year and reinvested the after-tax proceeds for the remaining four years.

At the end of year four, the proceeds would be $157,300 less cost of $100,000 for a gain of $57,300. Tax at 38% would be $21,770, and the reinvestment amount would be $157,300 less $21,770, or $135,530.

That $135,530 invested for the next four years would produce proceeds of $213,300. Cost would now be $135,530; the gain would be $77,770. Tax at 38% on the gain would be $29,550, to produce after-tax cash flow of $213,300 less $29,550 or $183,750.

Thus, the pure buy-and-hold strategy Donna selected generated close to $8,000 more in the end. This difference would be even bigger if more buying and selling occurred in the second option.

STRATEGY #15

Hold Tax-Disadvantaged Investments Inside Your RRSP or RRIF

Tax-disadvantaged investments are investment products that generate highly taxed income such as *interest* income. *Tax-advantaged* investments are investment products that generate dividends or capital gains — income that is taxed at lower rates than *interest.*

While trying to keep your overall *portfolio* balanced, consider holding interest-bearing investments inside your RRSP or RRIF and stocks and *equity mutual funds* outside your RRSP or RRIF. For individuals in the highest marginal tax bracket, this strategy can lower by up to 16% the income taxes paid on investment income every year. (Interest is taxed at 50%, while Canadian dividends and capital gains are taxed at 34% and 38% respectively.)

If you currently hold interest-bearing investments outside your RRSP or RRIF and stocks or equity mutual funds inside your RRSP or RRIF, consider switching them. Assuming you are dealing with investments of equal value and won't be throwing your current balanced investment portfolio out of whack, tell your investment advisor to switch the assets.

Note this common mistake: many Canadians employ the above strategy and transfer mutual funds with significant accrued gains attached into their RRSP. In that case, there is a *deemed disposition* on the investments on their transfer into the RRSP. That means any *accrued capital gains* on the mutual funds moved into the RRSP are realized and taxed on the transfer. The prospect of triggering this tax may cause individuals to re-evaluate the transfer of certain investments into their RRSP. Where possible, look to transfer assets without significant accrued capital gains, such as GICs or Canada Savings Bonds.

Some may argue that you should ignore the tax impact as described above because if you own an equity investment earning 15% annually and a GIC earning 5%, the overall tax deferral advantage from holding the equities inside the RRSP is more significant because of the larger return, and that I have my strategy backwards. My strategy is admittedly tax focused, and as I always state, tax should be only one factor to consider in the development of an investment portfolio. However, I would point out that my strategy is also risk focused, meaning that investors should consider holding their riskier investments (equities) outside their RRSP or RRIF, because the chances of earning 15% consistently may be low (and thus the tax factor becomes important again), and because there is the risk of loss with equities — and any losses realized outside an RRSP can be applied against other capital gains to reduce tax. Inside your RRSP an investment loss is just a loss of capital to you.

▼

Example

Jeff has $5,000 worth of *stripped bonds* outside his RRSP, invested for the long term (assume *fair market value* and cost are similar in this example, although this may not always be the case in reality). He also has a $20,000 RRSP consisting completely of equity mutual funds. With his investment advisor, Jeff completed an overall assessment of his appropriate *asset allocation mix* and determined that owning 80% equities was comfortable. The advisor suggested, however, that Jeff consider holding some of the fixed income component inside his RRSP, in order to benefit from the tax-advantaged nature of the equities. Jeff liked the idea of saving tax without changing his overall portfolio — instead, just reorganizing it! — and asked his investment advisor to switch $5,000 of equity funds in his RRSP with the $5,000 of stripped bonds.

This was a tax-smart move by Jeff for two reasons. First, future taxable investment income (primarily dividends and capital gains) arising from the equity mutual funds will be taxed at a lower rate than the stripped bond interest. Second, stripped bonds can be a poor investment outside an RRSP due to their structure. Stripped bonds provide their return only at maturity, but you must pay tax on the return annually. In other words, you have an annual tax expenditure, with no income inflows to pay the tax when due. This may leave you searching for ways to pay the tax bill.

One drawback of this strategy is that Jeff's stripped bonds are "deemed to be sold" prior to their transfer to the RRSP, and a small capital gain may be realized that will attract tax on Jeff's tax return next year. There is no tax bill in this case, though, and Jeff decided to proceed anyway. A larger potential tax liability might have caused Jeff to consider using some GICs for the RRSP transfer instead.

▼

Bonus Tip

A few words of caution about this strategy: before switching assets inside and outside your RRSP or RRIF, ensure that the move is consistent with your investment strategy and asset allocation. Also, ensure that factors such as your short-term cash needs are considered. Equity mutual funds may not be a good investment outside your RRSP or RRIF when you have a short-term cash crunch.

STRATEGY #16

Invest to Fight Inflation

Inflation is a term representing the increase in cost of living over time. Examples of the impact of inflation have been the rising cost of postage stamps, automobiles, and homes over the years. As the cost of living increases because of inflation, your income must also grow at the same pace in order to prevent a decrease in your standard of living.

When an individual buys a fixed income investment like a *GIC*, a rate of return is locked in for a period of time. During this same period of time, however, inflation continues to eat into *purchasing power*. For example, assume a GIC earning 6% annually is taxed at approximately 50% (for a Canadian in the top marginal tax bracket). This means that the after-tax return is only 3%. However, suppose that inflation in the same year is 3.5%. This means that the real rate of return on the GIC is – 0.5%. In other words, the investor lost ground. For people purchasing fixed income investments, this scenario is a real possibility.

There are, however, investments available that can fight inflation. Three examples are *dividend*-paying investments, rental properties, and indexed *bonds* (or real return bonds). Dividend income is generated by investment in stocks that pay dividends to shareholders. Mutual funds that invest in stocks may also pay dividend income. Many public companies, especially large *blue-chip* companies, pay dividends to their shareholders. Additionally, companies may regularly increase their dividend payments to shareholders. Many companies have long histories of raising dividend amounts. Raising dividend amounts is important because it offsets some or all of annual inflation and helps shareholders keep pace with the rising cost of living.

Rental income is the net profit that arises from owning a rental property or a *real estate investment trust.* (Real estate investment trusts are discussed in Strategy #21.) Rental income is a good inflation fighter since the income is derived from rents that people pay when they rent accommodations owned by an individual or a real estate investment trust. These rents generally increase over time (perhaps subject to rent controls) and thus an investor may receive an increasing amount of rent which keeps pace with inflation.

Indexed bonds are bond investments where the rate of return is regularly adjusted for an inflation factor.

From a tax point of view, rental properties and bonds generate *regular income* and interest income respectively, which are taxed at the least favourable rate in Canada. (A capital gain may also occur on the eventual sale of the investments, which would have a more favourable tax treatment.) Dividends are more favourably taxed and may be more desirable from a pure tax point of view.

Consider purchasing these types of investments as part of a well-balanced investment portfolio. Holding these type of assets can help you keep pace with inflation and guard against a decrease in your standard of living.

▼

Example

Dan is 65 and has been retired for 10 years already. He and his wife are living off his fixed income pension, some *non-registered* investments, and an RRSP in his wife's name which they haven't drawn on yet. In his 10 years of retirement, Dan has already noticed that he and his wife are finding it harder to stretch a dollar. He has realized that his fixed pension is buying less and less every year as inflation raises the cost of basic good and services. Even something as basic as the cost of riding the bus seems to be growing out of control.

Dan has been doing his own investing, and all of his portfolio is conservatively invested in GICs. Dan has never really thought about investing in anything else but thinks there must be more out there in terms of investments that will cost less in tax and increase his cash flow.

Recently, Dan's son introduced him to an investment advisor, Emma. Emma reviewed Dan's portfolio and noticed the fixed income investments. Appreciating his desire for low risk, Emma suggested that Dan take a small portion of his non-RRSP portfolio and purchase a good-quality, low-cost *blue-chip* dividend mutual fund. Dan agreed to part with an amount of money that he felt he could comfortably invest in the stock market, and permitted Emma to make the purchase on his behalf. Dan was committed for a five-year trial.

A year later, when Dan went to prepare his tax return, he noticed that some of his interest income was replaced this year with dividend income. He also noticed that his tax bill had shrunk in size, and he wondered why. He called Emma and she explained that dividend income is taxed at a much lower rate than interest income. Dan was pleased.

Some time after Dan filed his tax return, he noticed that the mutual fund distributions were getting slightly larger. He asked Emma why this was happening. She told him that sometimes the corporations paying the dividends raise the dividends for a variety of reasons. She pointed out that many of the largest corporations have a long history of regularly raising dividends. These increases in dividends serve as a good inflation fighter to keep an individual's income rising with the cost of living, and would help Dan to be able to afford the rising cost of taking the bus.

▼

Why Does a Dividend Fund Need to Be Low-Cost?

Dividends generated by investments in Canada typically amount to only a few percent of return each year. The return is enhanced by the favourable tax treatment offered for dividends. (See Strategy #17 for more information.) But with a low dividend distribution, these amounts can quickly be eaten up by a mutual fund with high management expenses (a high MER). For this reason, pay attention to cost of fund management with dividend funds, or consider supplementing the dividend funds with some direct ownership in high-quality, high-dividend-yielding shares.

One concern with high-dividend-paying investments (like utilities stocks, for example) is that they can be particularly sensitive to interest-rate changes. While they are desirable as inflation fighters, in periods of rising interest rates their share price may decrease. Why might interest rates rise? One reason is rising inflation! Keep this in consideration when investigating dividend-generating investments.

STRATEGY #17

Convert Some of Your Interest Income into Dividend Income

Individuals who need a steady flow of cash to help pay the bills believe that a large tax bill is the price they have to pay for safe and reliable *interest* income. But have these individuals ever considered *dividend* income? There can be quite a large difference in after-tax returns between interest and dividend income. One must earn approximately $132 in interest income to produce the same amount of after-tax income as $100 of dividends. This means that a 4.5% dividend may produce the same after-tax return as roughly 6% in interest income.

And what about *inflation* considerations? Interest-bearing investments pay a fixed rate of interest. The purchasing power of this interest income is reduced over time by inflation. This means that while a 6% *GIC* after-tax may pay only 3% to an investor, if inflation for that year was 4% then the investor actually lost ground on the investment — a – 1% real return! — since his or her dollar has less *purchasing power*.

Investors, including seniors, should consider holding some high-dividend-yielding *stocks*, or dividend-generating mutual funds that invest in high-yielding dividend stocks. Because these stocks are income oriented, management of the companies may also try to increase dividends regularly. Rising dividends provide a hedge against inflation that regular *bonds* and GICs usually don't offer. As well, outside an *RRSP* many Canadian dividend-generating investments can offer a great break on taxes.

Yes, purchasing stocks or stock mutual funds is more risky than buying GICs, but high-dividend-yielding stocks in Canada tend to be in utilities, resource companies, banks, and telephone companies. Several of these organizations are some of Canada's largest corporations and have a long history of paying dividends and increasing these dividends. To offset your concern about risk, purchase only an amount of stock or dividend-generating mutual funds that you are comfortable with.

As an added tax bonus, high-dividend-yielding stocks or dividend-generating mutual funds also offer the potential to earn capital gains from the increase in stock price owned directly or inside the mutual fund. Capital gains, like dividends, are *tax advantaged* compared to interest. Of course, stocks can sometimes result in capital losses as well!

One last tip: Canadians can purchase dividend-yielding stocks that typically pay in Canadian dollars, but Canadian-sourced dividends payable in foreign currencies like U.S. dollars also exist. Purchasing some of these foreign-pay investments allows additional diversification from foreign-currency exposure. These investments, being Canadian sourced, may also qualify for the preferential tax treatment afforded to taxable Canadian dividends.

▼

Example

Edward is 60, has retired, and dislikes completing his income tax return each year. It seems as though he is always paying more and more tax. Even worse, his accountant just told him that because of the large amount of interest income he earned last year, he will have to start paying income tax instalments as well. Edward needed the interest income to live on, but he doesn't like paying the related tax on the income. He is in the highest tax bracket, and at his marginal tax rate of 50%, he is keeping only half of his interest income. Edward asked his accountant if there was any planning he could consider to help his situation.

Edward's accountant explained the taxation of different types of investment income. Edward is particularly interested in the dividends, which at his marginal rate would be taxed at approximately 34% — much less than 50%. The accountant added that dividends would also fight inflation over time since dividends may be increased periodically by the company paying them.

The accountant referred Edward to a trusted and reliable investment advisor friend to learn more about dividends and to investigate dividend-paying investments. The investment advisor explained to Edward that he could create a portfolio of high-dividend-yielding stocks or he could purchase a dividend mutual fund. The investment advisor recommended the dividend fund because Edward didn't want to invest much money and many more companies can be invested in through a mutual fund when you have only a small amount of money to invest.

Edward could convert a small amount of his existing portfolio of interest-bearing GICs to dividend funds when the GICs mature, as a first step to replacing his interest income with dividend income. Over time, Edward might consider increasing this dividend-generating piece of his portfolio as he becomes more comfortable with dividends and dividend funds. Purchasing gradually over time would permit Edward to "test-drive" the products before buying them in any significant quantities and would keep his total investment portfolio at a level of risk he is comfortable with.

Crunching the Numbers

Edward's current portfolio and taxes:

$2,000,000	in GICs
5%	return last year
$100,000	total income
50%	tax rate
$50,000	**tax paid**
$50,000	**disposable income left**

Edward's potential portfolio and taxes, including some dividend-producing investments:

$1,500,000	in GICs
$500,000	in conservative dividend-yielding funds or stocks
$2,000,000	total portfolio
4.75%	return last year (5% on GICs, 4% on dividends)
$95,000	total income
46.63%	tax rate (50% on interest, 36% on dividends)
$44,300	**tax paid**
$50,700	**disposable income left**

With this mix of investments, Edward could increase his annual disposable income by $700.

For additional advice on dividends, see Strategy #16.

STRATEGY #18

Build Your Child's RRSP Before Age 18

Does your child (under age 18) have a paper route? Does your teenager work in retail? If they do, you probably don't file tax returns for them, because their total incomes are too low to attract any taxation. Why bother, right?

While you may enjoy the fact that they don't pay taxes on their income, you may not be aware that their *employment income* qualifies as *earned income* for purposes of determining RRSP contribution room. A child earning $1,000 a year in salary may also earn $180 of RRSP contribution room (18% of qualifying income annually). While that may not sound like a lot of money, remember that the child will likely not withdraw the funds from his or her RRSP for another 55 years. The power of compounding, assuming (say) an 8% rate of return annually, will turn that single $180 of contribution into $12,000 in 55 years.

Better still, the contribution to the RRSP can be made by you, the parent, and the money can be invested on behalf of the child inside his or her RRSP. Moreover, the related tax deduction does not have to be claimed by the child immediately and can be accumulated and claimed in the future when the child's income is significantly higher and he or she can get more benefit from the tax deduction.

This strategy permits the accumulation of valuable RRSP contribution room early in life, and can start the power of compounding investment income potentially 15 years earlier than your children might otherwise start contributing on their own.

▼

Example

Jane has a son, Tom, who is now in university. Since Tom was 12, he has worked at part-time jobs in the summer to provide himself with spending money. Each year Tom earned about $1,500, except last year, when he earned $8,000 before starting university. Tom's income is low enough that he hasn't had to pay any income taxes. However, five years ago his mother starting filing tax returns for him anyway, in order to start accumulating his RRSP contribution room.

Last year, when Tom turned 18, Jane contributed $1,980 to his RRSP to get him started on saving for the future. Like many young kids, Tom didn't have the cash to make a contribution himself. By starting Tom's RRSP at age 18 instead of something more common like age 28, Jane ensured that the $1,980 deposited at that time and earning 8% compounded annually will grow to $108,000 by the time Tom is 69, compared to only $50,000 if the RRSP had been started at age 28.

▼

Bonus Tip

If you think this is a great strategy but have not been filing tax returns for your children for the past few years when you could have been, take note: you may be able to go back and file for the last three years. Filing tax returns for your children for the last three years will permit you to establish their earned income for RRSP purposes and build their RRSP contribution room. Consult a tax advisor about filing or amending previous tax returns.

STRATEGY # 19

Investigate Oil and Gas Royalty Trusts

Oil and gas royalty income trusts have become a popular investment recently. Here is a summary of observations about their characteristics and their pros and cons, to help you understand them better.

- Oil and gas royalty income trusts are investment funds that permit *unit holders* (investors) to share in the production from oil and natural gas reserves. The future net cash flows earned from oil and gas production and sales are paid to such a trust as royalties. The trust may distribute most of the royalties it receives as cash distributions to unit holders.
- The revenue received in the trust can be reduced by special tax deductions available to resource operations and the result is that part or all of the cash flow distributed by the trust in the initial years is treated as a capital distribution (a return of the original investment) of the trust which is not subject to tax when received by the investor. Rather, the capital receipts reduce the cost base

of the investor's trust units and may result in a larger capital gain on the eventual sale of the units. Many investors incorrectly assume that the distributions are all income and simply attract a lower level of taxation. The amount of tax payable on this investment can increase as the level of income distributed to the unit holder increases, and also when the units are eventually sold by the unit holder. This means that these trusts offer a *deferral of tax* when owned outside an RRSP, and a potential capital gain on the sale of the units in the future.

- The trust is producing oil and gas from a depleting resource; in essence, an investor's capital is being returned with the production. If the trust does not replenish the oil and gas reserves with new properties, improve production methods, or benefit from increased prices, the investor may be left with nothing in the future. After all, the trust unit holder has no guarantee that the oil wells will continue to produce.
- Consumers should be cautious when comparing these returns to traditional *bond* or other fixed income investment returns. Oil and gas trusts can be affected by risks such as oil and gas price changes, market fluctuations, and declining production. These factors and others can affect distributions and the value of the trust units. This means that an oil and gas trust unit can behave more like an equity investment than a fixed income bond, and may need to be evaluated in that light by you in completing an assessment of risk and return for your investments. Another factor to consider when comparing returns is that the quoted annual returns of these trusts may include the return of capital, which is not an *earned* return, while other investments will quote only income returns.
- Other factors that can be important to a trust's market value are the reserve life of the oil and gas properties, the quality of the reserves, the rate of decline of the reserves,

and what portion of the investment return is a return of capital. Changes in these and other variables may lead to increases or decreases in the market value of units, resulting in a potential capital gain or loss if the investment is sold.

Oil and gas trusts can serve investors seeking an income tax deferral for a period of time. They can also serve investors in need of large cash distributions, but the investors must realize that the life of the oil and gas reserves is not guaranteed and therefore nor are the cash distributions.

Oil and gas trusts, along with several other variations of income trusts, are very popular today. They are complex investment vehicles which can carry some risk. Ensure that you talk to a qualified professional advisor with access to research on the products you are considering, who has access to a wide range of products for comparison and has a strong understanding of the tax, cash-flow, and investment ramifications of these products. Because an oil and gas trust defers tax, it is important that you understand the tax impact over the years you own the product — including the tax impact when you eventually sell.

Do your homework on these relatively new investments; don't get blinded by the flashy returns and apparently low tax bite!

▼

Example

Josh has a large, well-balanced investment portfolio outside his RRSP, consisting of bonds, a variety of mutual funds, some *stocks*, and some *GICs*. He has accumulated these savings from a large inheritance of $200,000 a few years back.

Recently Josh has been upset about the low interest rates

available for his maturing GICs. He has heard of oil and gas royalty trusts and their potential for higher returns. Their potentially lower tax bill is also attractive. Josh's investment advisor, Mike, advised on royalty trusts as an alternative to some stocks investments. Josh was ready to consider purchasing some trusts and started to investigate. Josh compared several oil and gas trusts, examining the quality of the management, life of reserves, and other aspects suggested by his investment advisor.

Portfolio *diversification* and tax minimization are important to Josh, but they are not the most important aspects of his investments. With a far-off retirement horizon, Josh has little need for the higher current distributions offered by the trusts. He decided to purchase a small amount of royalty trust units, limiting his purchase to approximately 5% of his overall portfolio — enough to get some tax deferral and additional investment diversification, but not so much as to increase portfolio risk beyond a level he is comfortable with. Because of the limited size of his purchase, Josh was comfortable with the risk exposure and was happy he still had the ability to achieve some tax deferral.

STRATEGY #20

Research Investing in Labour Funds

Labour-sponsored venture capital corporations ("*labour funds*") offer yet another asset class for a diversified portfolio: venture capital. Labour funds, which operate much like mutual funds, have been approved by the federal and provincial governments for the purposes of making investments into private businesses in Canada.

To attract investors, labour funds can offer significant *tax credits*: up to 15% of the amount invested (to a maximum investment of $3,500) is rebated by the federal government and often another 15% by some provincial governments (these credit amounts can vary). Since these same labour funds may also be eligible for your RRSP, they offer an additional 50% *tax deduction* to investors in the top tax bracket in Canada, reducing the cost of a $3,500 investment to $700. The trade-off is that investors are often required to hold these investments for a minimum time period or else lose the federal and provincial tax credits, and the investments can be somewhat riskier.

When evaluating labour funds for purchase, consider the

following: if you stripped away the attractive tax benefits, would the investment stand on its own merits? Like mutual funds, there are newer labour funds and there are older labour funds, and you should examine past *performance* carefully — but not solely. Remember, past performance may not be an indication of future performance, so it is also important to understand future potential of the fund. Note that *investment risk* associated with labour funds can be high; some funds invest in emerging, young, private companies in search of money, companies that may not be able to obtain the funding any other way. When evaluating labour funds for purchase, review the risk level with your financial advisor and ensure that the amount of risk assumed is consistent with your preferences.

As when evaluating all managed investment products, you should be concerned with the quality of management. Management should be experienced and qualified to manage such a fund. Read the labour fund's *prospectus* to gather some background information on the fund management team. Other information can be obtained by talking to your investment advisor. Don't be afraid to ask questions!

And then there are fees and costs of the labour fund. Like in a mutual fund, the fund management charges the fund a fee to operate and manage it. This fee can be steep in some cases, due sometimes to the additional legwork required for management to find and investigate new private business opportunities. There may also be a diminishing redemption fee associated with selling a fund after a short ownership period. And there could be a loss of tax credits if the funds are sold early. Investigate all of the fees associated with the particular labour fund(s) you are interested in buying.

Labour funds can produce a sizable tax deduction for your RRSP and some desirable tax credits as well, but purchase amounts should be well thought out. Don't lose sight of the importance of the investment just because of a tax write-off. Investigate the quality of the investment before buying. This type of investment can be a welcome part of a balanced investment portfolio, but do your homework before buying and consider seeking the advice of a qualified investment and tax advisor to assist you with the decision.

▼

Example

Marian was shopping for her RRSP investments in February two years ago, and the significant tax breaks associated with labour-sponsored venture capital funds were hard to ignore. She was sold on the large tax credits offered in addition to the RRSP deduction. Marian really dislikes giving Revenue Canada any money, so these investments seemed like a good option. Marian bought $3,500 worth of one fund that year and another $3,000 the next year. This year, Marian is pondering the purchase of another labour fund investment, to add to her existing holdings in her $12,000 RRSP.

Looking back on last year, Marian now sees that she got caught up in the tax savings and ignored the investments behind the tax write-off of her labour fund. That year, the *TSE 300* returned 28%, while her two labour funds returned significantly less. Much of her tax savings from the initial investment were offset in one year of poor performance. Furthermore, she can't even switch funds now because of the redemption fees and loss of credits if she sells the labour fund early. So now she is concerned that these higher-risk investments will continue to underperform versus the markets and cost her more and more in opportunity cost each year. She is concerned that she may never have enough for retirement at this rate.

Marian's new financial advisor pointed out to her that a labour fund should be viewed as a long-term investment and that returns may be volatile based on the risk level of the fund. He suggested that Marian wait another three to five years to assess the performance of the funds fairly. Her existing labour funds had been selected without any research at all, and without any consideration for *risk tolerance* and the rest of her investment portfolio. He suggested that this year, Marian should consider balancing her total RRSP portfolio by adding some bonds and blue-chip equity mutual funds according to a risk assessment and asset mix they could design together. He stated, however, that labour funds can form a suitable piece of a well-balanced investment portfolio. They could even consider purchasing some additional labour funds this year, after a thorough evaluation of Marian's needs and alternatives.

STRATEGY #21

Diversify into Real Estate Investment Trusts

Real estate investment trusts or REITs are publicly traded *closed-end trusts* or *trusts* that own, operate, acquire, and develop or finance real estate properties. "Closed-end" means that unlike in a mutual fund trust, there is a limit on the availability of the trust units. Most REITs invest in private and commercial real estate ranging from residential properties and regional malls to office, industrial, and health care properties. Here is a list of some of their characteristics, to assist you if you are considering a REIT purchase:

- Liquidity — Unlike pure real estate investments, publicly traded REITs trade on *stock exchanges*, making them much easier to sell than a single rental property.
- Diversification — Owning a REIT or several REITs means that you may own a share of properties across a region, a country, or a continent, helping to cushion the effect of suddenly depressed market conditions which may occur in any one area. This diversification may be preferable to owning one property in only one city.

- Effective management of the REIT — Many U.S. REITs are fully functioning businesses, with management owning a percentage of the outstanding shares. Many Canadian REITs still hire management on a fee basis. Ownership by management can mean a greater devotion by management to be successful.
- Inflation fighter and a growth investment — REITs are a separate asset class and add effective diversification to a *stock* and *bond* portfolio. Rising rents and growing property values make REITs a growth investment and an *inflation* fighter.
- Defensive investing strengths — REITs are a good defensive choice in a rising or high stock market; because of high cash yields, they hold their value better in down markets. REITS are, however, subject to changes in interest rates, market growth, and real estate markets, and are not guaranteed investments.
- Some tax deferral — A portion of Canadian REIT distributions can be tax deferred as a result of capital cost allowance claimed by the REIT. Capital cost allowance is a notional non-cash expense to represent usage of a property (known as depreciation for accounting purposes). The capital cost allowance reduces taxable income but doesn't affect cash distributions to the *unit holder*. Unfortunately, this same capital cost allowance is applied to reduce the cost base of the investment, potentially resulting in a capital gain on the eventual sale of the investment. But at least it may be a *tax-advantaged* capital gain! In addition, the capital cost allowance claim may result in *recapture*, which is taxed as *regular income* when the individual real estate property is sold.
- Ownership of a non-depleting asset — With oil and gas royalty trusts, the properties indirectly owned by the trusts are depleted. With REITs, on the other hand, you have a permanent investment that can continue to pay

rental income and also have potential for capital growth on the value of the investment.

- A low-hassle investment — Professional management teams run REITs and the investments they hold. Compare this to rental properties, where you might be out cutting the grass every other week!
- REITs are structured as trusts, not *corporations* — This leaves investors at risk of unlimited liability in the case of any large lawsuits against REIT properties. Check that the REIT management has property, casualty, and liability insurance as well as effective investing policies and other safeguards in place to minimize investor exposure to loss.

Like other stock market investments, REITs will fluctuate in value over time. The value of a REIT should be evaluated on all its merits and faults by you and a financial advisor experienced in REITs. Consider consulting a tax professional in order to completely understand the tax impact of REITs during the period you will own one (if held outside an RRSP), and the tax impact on *disposal* of such an investment.

▼

Example

John was interested in adding some real estate to his non-RRSP investment portfolio and was considering purchasing a rental apartment building. John already had a large portfolio and felt the addition of real estate in some form would be *diversification* into an asset class he didn't currently hold. This added diversification, plus the inflation-fighting ability offered by the potential for rising rental income (through higher rents), was attractive. John admitted to his investment advisor, however, that he wanted a "low-maintenance" investment. The advisor said that owning his own rental property would require maintenance and upkeep, unless he was prepared to use a management company, which could prove costly. When the investment advisor noted that the disadvantages of personal real estate ownership include potentially poor liquidity if the property is hard to sell, and the uncertainty of performance of regional real estate markets, John decided to reconsider his purchase of his own real estate investment. Owning a rental property was attractive, but didn't seem to fit his lifestyle.

John wasn't aware of REITs until his investment advisor told him about them. John was attracted to the pros and could live with the cons of a Canadian REIT, and made a purchase for his portfolio after researching REITs with his advisor. The REIT seemed to offer all the advantages of a single rental property with few of the disadvantages. John's investment advisor had told him that owning a REIT would diversify his investment portfolio, would act as an inflation fighter, and might prove to be a growth investment. The REIT would be a growth investment if the rental properties owned by the REIT appreciated in value over time and this value was reflected in an increased value of John's REIT investment.

When John was shopping for a REIT investment, his advisor discussed the advantages of owning REITs investing in a variety of properties, in a variety of regions in a country, and even in several countries. If this diversification was not available from one REIT, the advisor suggested purchasing more than one REIT. The REIT that John and the advisor chose invested across Canada, providing exposure to several diverse real estate markets. John and the investment advisor also inquired about management quality, and compared the fee levels of several REITs before John purchased.

Finally, they investigated the extent to which *leveraging* or borrowed money was used to purchase investments in the

REIT. They were concerned that the REIT might borrow excessively in order to purchase more properties. John and his advisor examined the REIT's financial statements and were satisfied that the REIT's leverage was not excessive. This opinion of the leverage was reaffirmed by discussions with the REIT management and John's accountant.

As with any investment, shop around for the best prices, and understand the differences among REITs in the marketplace. A REIT investment is an option for a well-balanced investment portfolio seeking diversification into an additional asset class.

STRATEGY #22

Take Advantage of Dividend Reinvestment Plans and Direct Share Ownership

Individuals who purchase an *equity mutual fund* purchase a collection of investments consisting primarily of *stocks* of public companies. So have you ever thought about owning those same stocks directly? Why not bypass most of the fees? Why not take advantage of free subsequent purchases?

Investing in stocks directly has several advantages. First, it eliminates the fees that your mutual fund manager charges you each year for managing your mutual fund *portfolio* (both the *load* fee and the internal fund *MER*). This alone may increase your rate of return 2% every year that you own shares directly. Second, you can purchase the stock investment fresh; in other words, your purchase price is your cost, and any future appreciation is earned by you and you pay tax on it. With mutual funds, you buy fund units which hold existing investments — investments which may have accrued capital gains you didn't earn but may pay tax on when sold (see Strategy #4). Third, you control the timing of the taxes associated with any capital gains you earn. With a mutual fund, your fund manager buys and sells stock when he or she wants to, and you face the tax liability when this happens. But if you purchase the stock directly and practise a *buy-and-hold* strategy, you can defer any capital gains until you decide to sell.

Yet another benefit of buying a company's stock directly is that you may be able to get involved in *dividend reinvestment plans* offered by the company. This is where any dividends you earn can be automatically reinvested to purchase more shares. While you still have to pay tax on these dividends, remember that dividend income is *tax-advantaged* income: outside your RRSP you will pay less tax on dividend income compared to other types of income. Reinvesting dividends can be a powerful investment strategy because the reinvestment compounds the growth of your investment at an increasing rate as each year more dividends are earned and reinvested. Note that reinvestment of dividends is also available with mutual funds.

Thus, the strategy of buying shares directly has its merits, but here is a word of caution: buying mutual funds is usually more appropriate for investors who don't have enough money to purchase a diversified portfolio of stocks directly. Buying only a few stocks is far more risky than purchasing a mutual fund which may hold a diversified portfolio of 40 or more stocks. So what should you do? Well, if you really want to own some *equities*, consider buying shares in a few of the big blue-chip companies in Canada that constitute lower-risk investments and offer dividend reinvestment plans. Speak to your investment advisor about a sample of these types of stocks.

And one other word of caution: while buying stocks directly can be a less expensive method of investing, in many cases it comes without professional investment advice. Depending on your investing sophistication, an investment advisor may add value by assisting you in evaluating what to buy, and when to eventually sell.

▼

Example

Outside his RRSP, Trevor had a diversified portfolio of bonds and mutual funds totalling $500,000. He wanted to use part of this money and invest in some specific stocks that he believed would be solid long-term investments. Using his investment advisor, he purchased 1,000 shares in ABC Bank (paying a 2% commission to do so) and had the shares registered in his name so that he personally could enrol in the company's dividend reinvestment plan and optional *share purchase program.*

Normally, shares purchased through investment advisors and their firms are held in *street name* (not your name), and dividend reinvestment and additional share purchases made directly from the company may not be available. Why would your investment advisor want to give you access to free purchase? Some brokerages do offer free dividend reinvestment, however.

Trevor was also attracted to the optional share purchase program offered by his new investment in the bank. His advisor pointed out that many public companies in Canada (and many more in the U.S.) permit investors to make additional cash contributions to the company directly to purchase more shares with no fees. This is a great feature; some companies even let investors buy additional shares at a discount to market value.

The low fee cost of his new investment is appealing to Trevor, but the new record-keeping responsibilities are not. Since he owns the stock directly, he is also responsible for the administrative burden of keeping track of purchases, sales, reinvestments, and the tax cost base of the investment. Owning this same investment through a brokerage account might have reduced this burden, since it likely has a computerized record-keeping system in place. But because Trevor has only one stock investment owned directly, he doesn't think the paperwork should be overwhelming. In the future, though, he will evaluate this administrative burden against the fee savings when considering his preferred purchase route.

STRATEGY #23

Use Prescribed Annuities for Tax Deferral

An *annuity* is a stream of payments received by an individual for a period of time. Individuals can purchase annuities with a lump sum of money that will be used to provide the stream of payments in the future.

An annuity can be a particularly effective investment for several reasons. First, owning an annuity requires little if any maintenance. The amount of the future payments is set when the annuity is purchased and no further investment management is required by the investor. For seniors, for example, getting a cheque every month may be the only involvement they desire in managing their investments. Using annuities to provide low-hassle retirement income can reduce the stress of investing for many people, by simplifying their financial picture.

Second, a *prescribed annuity* can provide a deferral of tax, particularly in the annuity's first few years. Each annuity payment received is a blend of interest income and a return of the invested money. With a regular annuity, a greater amount of taxable interest is received early in the term of the annuity. With a prescribed annuity, the taxable interest is spread equally over the life of the annuity, thereby deferring the payment of tax compared to the case of a regular annuity. For a senior who may be on a fixed income who is concerned about taxes, a prescribed annuity can provide an improved cash flow in the early years of receiving annuity payments.

Third, an annuity can be useful as an investment that restricts control of itself by beneficiaries who may lack control over their spending habits. For an individual who is concerned that his or her children may spend every penny of the *estate*, an annuity can be a low-cost way to deal with that concern. An individual can direct his or her estate to purchase a life annuity (an annuity that provides payments for the entire life of the beneficiaries). With a life annuity, the beneficiaries will receive a regular income stream but can never access the principal amount. This strategy can also be useful for providing for medically challenged dependants who may not be capable of managing their personal affairs.

It is important to note that the cost of an annuity may fluctuate with changes in interest rates. Consider looking into annuities when market interest rates are higher, as this may result in less expensive annuity costs and higher payments to the beneficiaries. Also, annuities come in several shapes and sizes — e.g., you can purchase an annuity that raises payments to adjust for inflation — and can be purchased from a variety of institutions. Investigate annuities carefully and thoroughly before deciding whether to buy, including doing an analysis of the size and stability of the company offering the annuity. (Remember, the payments may have to last 50 years!)

If you decide to purchase a large annuity for your needs, consider buying two annuities from two institutions to address your concerns about the risks of having all your money with one institution.

▼

Example

Ben and Rose have been talking to their financial advisor about simplifying their personal finances. At ages 77 and 79 respectively, they no longer have the desire to stay as involved in the regular decision making relating to their investments.

This change of heart has been partly due to Ben's stroke six months ago. Ben had been the financial decision maker for the family, and since his stroke Rose has been concerned about his reduced desire and ability to focus on their family cash flows. They thought about asking their children for help, but the children live far away and Ben and Rose don't want to burden them. They would simply like to reduce their involvement in investment decision making.

Dana, their advisor, suggested that Ben and Rose consider purchasing a prescribed annuity with their taxable investments, while continuing to manage their tax-sheltered funds as *RRIFs*. She explained what an annuity is and what the advantages will be to Ben and Rose:

- The annuity will provide a level stream of payments on a regular basis that can help to provide Ben and Rose with the regular cash flow they need to live.
- The annuity is managed by an insurance company. Once Ben and Rose provide a lump-sum amount to purchase the annuity, they will have no ongoing management responsibility. The insurance company will provide them with regular payments according to the terms of the annuity. This arrangement meets Ben and Rose's desire to have less investment responsibility.
- The after-tax cash flow to Ben and Rose may increase in the short term since the annuity payments will consist of some income and a return of original capital. The capital

portion is not taxed. This additional cash flow will come in handy to pay for the expensive medical attention Ben is receiving as a result of his stroke.

Dana noted that many people worry about the continued solvency of Canadian insurance companies that sell annuities. While this is always a concern, she explained that they could purchase the annuity from one of Canada's largest institutions, or they could purchase two annuities from two different institutions, to further diversify and reduce risk of loss.

Finally, Dana suggested that Ben and Rose invest only a portion of the funds in an annuity. Like other types of investment, an annuity is an option where you may want to invest some money, but not necessarily all your money. A small investment will provide Ben and Rose with the many advantages of an annuity but will not leave them locked in with only one type of investment. Dana observed that Ben and Rose will continue to own RRIFs with their tax-sheltered investments, and Dana can continue to assist them in managing this part of their finances.

Rose liked this balanced approach. It would be less work for them. She wants to start looking at different annuity options immediately.

STRATEGY #24

Replace Mutual Funds with Pooled Fund Investments

Pooled funds are similar to mutual funds but have higher minimum investment amounts. Pooled funds are consequently far less known in Canada than mutual funds, because the former are not available to the average Canadian. The minimum investment of at least $150,000 per fund is significantly higher than for mutual funds, which may have a minimum investment of $1,000. However, if you are someone with a growing investment portfolio or will likely inherit some wealth later in life, pooled funds may make sense for you as a replacement or supplement to your mutual fund portfolio.

Consider this: the average annual *management expense ratio* (MER) of an equity mutual fund in Canada is currently over 2%. And add to this any purchase or sale loads you might also pay associated with the mutual fund.

Now consider this: several pooled equity funds in Canada have MERs of approximately 1% or less, with no load fees. This means that you could own a similar investment, with a 1% saving every year! On a $100,000 investment in a pooled fund, you will save $1,000 every single year! This $1,000 savings, when compounded at 8% for 30 years, will grow to $113,000!

Aside from their cost savings, many of the pooled funds currently available in Canada are available on a no-load basis. That is, there may be no fees to buy or sell such a fund. Despite fee and expense differences, pooled funds can hold the same investments as mutual funds and operate in a similar fashion. Some of the mutual fund companies you currently invest in may also offer pooled funds, and you may not know it!

A word on diversification and pooled funds: proper *asset allocation* strategies involve investing across several asset classes: Canadian equities, international equities, bonds, etc. Since pooled funds have a minimum investment per fund of at least $150,000, an investor likely needs at least $500,000 to develop a properly balanced portfolio of pooled funds. However, a pooled fund can be combined with mutual funds to achieve diversification more easily but potentially at a greater cost.

Investors who meet the minimum investment levels should consider pooled fund investments. Chances are, the mutual fund companies they currently invest with also have pooled funds consisting of similar investments.

▼

Example

Jody is just getting over the passing away of her father several months ago. Since he was predeceased by her mother, Jody now finds herself the sole beneficiary of their estate. In two weeks the family lawyer is sending her a cheque for $700,000 to cover the cash component of the estate. Jody approached her *financial planner* about options for investing the money.

Jody was going to buy mutual funds, until her financial planner introduced her to pooled funds. She learned that she could purchase them without any upfront fees, switching fees, or deferred fees. Even better, she liked the fact that annual management expenses of the funds were generally 1% or 1.5% — compared to 2% or 2.5% for regular mutual funds.

After she completed a risk assessment and developed a proper asset allocation mix, Jody and the financial planner reviewed several companies offering pooled funds, before settling on two. Jody decided to divide her money between two companies in order to reduce the risk of putting all of her money in one basket. Also, since each manager looked at investing in a different way, the division would further reduce risk. That way, one manager might have a good year while the other has a bad year, but with the combination Jody would be less likely to have a bad year overall. Investing with only one manager would increase the likelihood that Jody would have a bad investment year at some point in the future.

The financial planner smiled and together they proceeded to investigate the process of investing with these two pooled fund managers.

Crunching the Numbers

Given Jody's $700,000, saving 1% on fees means an extra $3,500 after-tax in her pocket every year. Over 20 years, compounded annually at 8%, this will accumulate to $170,000 pre-tax. In other words, fees matter!

STRATEGY #25

Balance Your Investment Mix with Wrapped Products

Today in Canada, *wrapped investment products,* created mainly by the big brokerages, are becoming popular investments. There are two kinds: wrapped pooled products and segregated wrapped products. A wrapped product is an investment where a number of professional *money managers* have been contracted to manage a piece of an investment portfolio. There may be a Canadian equity manager, a Canadian bond manager, an international equity manager, and so on, and each manager may be from a different company. Additionally, the wrapped product may have several managers within each asset class, each managing a piece using his or her own style of investing. This differentiation in style is a form of additional diversification that can reduce your *investment risk.*

Investors purchasing a wrapped product will be assisted by an investment advisor to formulate a proper *asset allocation mix* based on risk and return profiles, and also may be able to select which managers (from a stable within the wrapped product) will manage their money.

A wrapped product may be sold with a single fee which may be tax deductible, and this fee can incorporate the transaction fees, custody fees, and any other costs associated with this product.

Here are some advantages of a wrapped product:

- Instead of having one money manager managing a fund, you may have access to several professional managers in one product. More diversification among many managers can reduce your investment risk.
- You are charged one annual fee based on the value of your investment. Fees based on the market value of the portfolio encourage the money manager to grow your wealth. This may be preferable to you owning stocks and bonds, where a broker gets paid for buying and selling on your behalf and may sell more frequently to generate more commissions.
- With a segregated wrapped product you are purchasing *segregated money management* as opposed to buying a pool or fund. This means that when you buy in, the investments inside your account are purchased fresh; you don't purchase a fund that may have accrued capital gains you didn't earn but may pay tax on — unlike those that may exist inside a mutual or pooled fund. (This only matters outside an RRSP or RRIF.)
- Reporting is generally good in a wrapped product. More of the wrapped products provide personal rates of return on your investment and a benchmark against which you can compare returns.
- Wrapped products are available to investors with less than $250,000, in some cases. Normally, investors need greater than $1 million to create a similar investment portfolio on their own.

Some disadvantages of a wrapped product include:

- Relatively high fees. The annual fee may be approximately 2% to 3% a year. Thus, on a $1,000,000 investment you may pay a fee of up to $30,000 each year. Do you feel like you are getting $30,000 worth of value every year? For that fee, you do get access to more than just an investment product. In most cases, a financial advisor will assist you to determine your appropriate asset allocation, discuss the appropriate money managers for you, and be available for your ongoing investment needs.
- Also with respect to fees, be aware that few professional money managers can beat the indices (like the TSE 300 and the S&P 500) consistently by 2–3%. If they can't beat an index, why not just buy an index fund investment (with typical fees of about 0.5%) and save all the fees?
- Many of the wrapped products available have hired good money managers, but perhaps not all the best managers available for a particular asset class. Some of the exceptional managers are not available through wrapped products.
- Because a wrapped product is custom made by the institution offering it, the investment may be difficult to transfer to another institution if you become unhappy with the present one. If you want to take your business elsewhere, you may have to dispose of your wrapped product and take the cash to your new advisor. Any selling of the wrapped account holdings outside of an RRSP or RRIF attracts tax, and this is not desirable. This forced selling isn't always necessary, and in many instances you can transfer your portfolio out "as is" without triggering any tax. You'll want to clarify the rules about leaving before you buy in the first place, and also ask if there are any exit fees.
- While segregated wrapped products are generally available to investors with small amounts to invest, criticism

can be made based on the difficulty a money manager may have in creating a properly diversified portfolio in a cost-effective way with less than $500,000. Better investment diversification may be available through mutual or pooled funds.

- Investors interested in having a close relationship with the money manager directly, instead of through a financial advisor representing the wrapped product, cannot have such a relationship with a wrapped product. While some institutions selling wrapped products will invite you to hear the money managers speak at seminars, this doesn't replace a personal relationship with the money manager who is investing your money.

If you are going to buy a wrapped product, shop around. Every institution seems to have one, each with a similar group of money managers and each with similar fees. Compare at least three wrapped products before buying in order to get a good understanding of each institution's process to invest your money in the wrap, the institution's commitment to customer service, and all the options of the products available. Decide whether the higher cost of these products is worth the pros and cons according to your personal needs.

▼

Example

Suzanne had just won $3 million in a lottery, and after recovering from the surprise of winning, she decided to invest most of her prize for the long term. She set out on her own to investigate professional money managers, mutual funds, pooled funds, and wrapped accounts for her investment needs.

After a series of interviews with some alternatives, Suzanne paused to review her notes:

Mutual Funds

- Mutual funds can be expensive investments when you consider loads and annual management expenses greater than 2% on average for Canadian equity funds.
- They offer broad diversification in dozens of asset classes, industries, and countries around the world.
- There are approximately 1,600 funds to pick from in Canada, providing adequate choice to create a tailor-made investment portfolio.

My mutual fund conclusion: not for my $3 million. Mutual funds are one of the most expensive types of managed money, partly because they deal with small client amounts which are expensive to administer. With my $3 million, I have greater bargaining power to ask for lower fees and there are more products available to me that are tailored for high-net-worth investors.

Pooled Funds

- Pooled funds have the same diversification advantages as mutual funds but with lower fees.
- Minimum investment amounts are $150,000.
- There are fewer funds to pick from in Canada, but still adequate selection exists and more funds are being developed all the time.
- They have the same tax disadvantages as mutual funds, where an investor purchases a pool of investments which may contain accrued capital gains he or she may pay tax on at some point when the investment is sold inside the fund and the gain is flowed out to unit holders.

My pooled fund conclusion: pooled and mutual funds offer broad *diversification*, which is valuable to me. Pooled funds can be bought from top managers for approximately 1% per year. That means an approximate savings in fees of 1% every year over average Canadian equity mutual funds. But tax matters to me, so I'll investigate segregated money management, where money managers create my own portfolio of stocks and bonds.

Segregated Wrapped Products

- Segregated wrapped products are attractive because of their tax advantages — stocks are bought new when I invest and I pay tax only on my *own* capital gains.
- They are also attractive because of the diversification resulting from the multiple money managers.
- A fee of 2% would be an annual fee of $60,000 for investment management on my $3 million. Surely I can get adequate investment management for less than this?

My segregated wrapped product conclusion: The cost is high, but I like the reduced risk through being able to invest with many money managers inside the wrapped product.

Segregated Money Management with a Professional Money Manager Directly (Unwrapped)

- Segregated money management involves money managers who create my own account of stocks and bonds. That means I get all new investments and no tax disad vantages of buying funds with accrued capital gains and potential future tax liabilities (problems which I would with mutual funds and pooled funds). And I get some of the same money managers who are used in the segregated wrapped products.
- Since I have $3 million, I could invest $1.5 million with each of two money managers who use different investment

styles, for added diversification. Two managers are better than one, but may not be as good as four or more, each managing a piece of my portfolio using his or her own style and specialization. But do I really need four?
- Each money manager will provide an account manager to service my ongoing investment needs and complete an appropriate investment plan for me. I like having two, because they will act as second opinions to each other.
- I don't get the comprehensive reporting package that a wrapped product offers, but I'm comfortable getting a *performance* statement from each manager and dealing with an account manager for each company.
- Each money manager will generally charge me well below 2% annually.

My segregated money management conclusion: these managers will manage my money for a low annual cost and still provide diversification. For me, the lower fees matter, yet I want more diversification.

My overall conclusion: I think I'll place $2 million of my money with two segregated account managers and place $500,000 in a segregated wrapped account. With the other $500,000 I will top up my RRSP using index mutual funds and keep the remainder fairly liquid for spending needs. This way, I get broad diversification from reputable organizations at an overall reasonable cost, and I don't have all my money at risk with only one organization.

STRATEGY #26

Weigh TIPS Investments for Your Equity Needs

Have you considered some *TIPS* as an investment alternative to equity funds and equity index funds? TSE 35 Index Participation Units or "TIPS" are created by the *Toronto Stock Exchange* to permit investors to own a piece of the TSE 35 Index. The TSE 35 Index consists of some of the largest and most heavily traded publicly listed companies in Canada and is a subset of the TSE 300. Ownership of the TSE 35 offers diversification geographically and across industries; it offers liquidity, as the units are easy to sell; and the TSE 35 Index offers the flow through of dividends paid by the companies owned by the units. Most of the 35 companies included in the TIPS index have a *market capitalization* greater than $1 billion, meaning that the TSE 35 is a holding of *blue-chip* Canadian *equities.* Over the period from February 1992 to February 1997, the annual return with dividends reinvested in TIPS has been 14.6%.

Since the Toronto Stock Exchange promises to cover all excessive management costs that may reduce an investor's yield, a TIPS investment has the benefits of a blue-chip mutual fund without the annual management fees (which currently average over 2% per year for Canadian equity funds). And since TIPS are fully invested in the index, there are no *money managers* required behind the scenes to buy and sell stocks. This means no worries about managers possibly leaving the fund.

TIPS pay dividends quarterly. Incoming dividends are held in an interest-bearing account until they are paid out, with the interest earned on the account going to pay administrative costs of operating TIPS. The Toronto Stock Exchange covers all unpaid expenses. Regular mutual funds pay all fees out of your returns, and also take a profit component for the fund company, all of which can together approach 3% a year. TIPS have no ongoing fees.

The TIPS *portfolio* is adjusted to reflect the changes in the TSE 35 Index. Historically, there have not been many changes in the composition of the index, meaning that turnover in your TIPS portfolio should be low — attracting less tax from fewer realized capital gains.

An additional note: TIPS have a brother called "HIPS," which are a similar investment created by the Toronto Stock Exchange to invest in the top 100 companies in the TSE 300 Index. HIPS operate in a similar fashion to TIPS, except that you can obtain broader diversification since HIPS invest across 100 large companies in a variety of industries.

Similar investments exist in the United States' stock markets as well. All of these investments represent excellent low-cost methods of purchasing a play on the major indices or portions of the major indices in Canada and elsewhere.

▼

Example

George owns several Canadian equity mutual funds inside his RRSP. Every February, George picks another fund for the Canadian equity component of his RRSP investment. This year, George has discovered TIPS, and he plans to purchase them for his *discount brokerage* account. He likes the diversified blue-chip portfolio offered by TIPS. He also likes the fact that there is no worry about a manager leaving the fund company. But most of all, he likes the cost savings, which work out as follows:

Estimated brokerage fee to purchase 300 TIPS units (300 units x $30/unit x 1%)	$90
Annual management cost of the portfolio	$0
Total year-one fee to own TIPS	**$90**
Total future fees to own TIPS	**$0**

Purchase price (2% front load) of a similar equity mutual fund (300 units x $30/unit x 2%)	$180
Annual management cost of the portfolio (300 units x $30/unit x 2.25%)	$203
Total year-one fee to own the fund	**$383**
Total future fees to own the fund	**$203/year**

STRATEGY #27

Replace Some GICs with Stripped Bonds

Guaranteed Investment Certificates or GICs are investments that provide a fixed amount of interest over a fixed period of time. They are generally not cashable prior to maturity, and may be guaranteed to some extent by the Canadian Deposit Insurance Corporation (*CDIC*).

Government *stripped bonds* are obligations of the federal or provincial government that are created when the semi-annual interest payments (the coupons) of a bond are separated from the bond itself to create two investment products from one. The separated bond coupon payments and the residual bond sell at a discount to their maturity value, and on maturity they pay out their maturity value. Both the coupon payments and the residue have come to be known as "stripped bonds."

There are no income distributions during the life of the separated coupons or residue, but rather the purchase amount increases in value annually until the maturity value is reached. This increase in value over a period of time determines the yield to maturity or the rate of return on the stripped bonds.

Note that for tax purposes, income in the form of accruing yield from the coupons or the residue is taxed annually, even though no actual income distributions are received until maturity (when the maturity value of the investment is received). This can create problems for individuals relying on timely income distributions to pay the tax due on the annual return. This negative tax aspect can make purchasing stripped bonds outside an RRSP unattractive.

There are several reasons why you should consider purchasing stripped bonds for your RRSP:

- Safety. Stripped government bonds offer the same credit rating and level of safety provided by a regular federal government or provincial government bond. This means that stripped bonds offer a full guarantee of principal and interest to maturity and likely come with an independent credit rating as to the quality of the bonds. Guaranteed Investment Certificates, however, may be guaranteed only up to $60,000 under the Canadian Deposit Insurance Corporation.
- Higher interest rate. The interest earned on a stripped bond may be higher than that on a GIC of comparable term. This is due to the fact that stripped bonds, unlike GICs, are traded in an open market, and within this market there is a wider variety of issuers with different characteristics, all of which have varying credit ratings, which impact return. Also, GIC interest rates, which are set by the institutions offering them, may not change as quickly as the Canadian bond market, which reacts immediately to factors warranting a change in value.
- *Liquidity.* Stripped bonds trade in the secondary market in Canada, and can be bought and sold relatively easily on a daily basis. Stripped bonds are not locked in until maturity, and they have good liquidity if you need the money. GICs, on the other hand, are locked-in investments.

- Tax advantages. GICs earn interest income, which is the most *tax-disadvantaged* type of income available in Canada. Stripped bonds earn interest income too, but have the potential to produce *tax-advantaged* capital gains and capital losses. (Tax advantage is not relevant inside an RRSP, however.) A capital gain or loss depends on what happens to interest rates in the marketplace after the bond is purchased. If rates fall after the bond is purchased, the bond becomes more attractive. This raises the market value of the stripped bond and a capital gain is possible if the bond is sold prior to maturity. On the negative side, the absence of regular interest income associated with regular bonds means that the value of stripped bonds is more volatile in relation to interest-rate changes in the marketplace. A rise in interest rates may result in a capital loss if the stripped bond is sold prior to maturity.
- Flexibility. GICs are typically available in up to five-year terms. Stripped bonds are available with terms ranging from less than a year to greater than 25 years. Stripped bonds can be tailored to a variety of investment needs through a combination of different maturities and face values. A stripped bond *portfolio* can be set up to have a bond mature in year one, year two, and so on, such that an entire portfolio can be structured to provide annual retirement income each year as needed. Additionally, a laddered portfolio as described can also be renewed over a period of time so that a large amount of the portfolio is never faced with reinvestment during a period of low interest rates.
- No reinvestment risk. Since stripped bonds don't pay anything before maturity, there is no worrying about how to reinvest income generated from the investment. This is unlike the situation with regular bonds, where an investor can find widely different interest-rate conditions

in the marketplace when it comes time to decide what to do with the interest income generated each year from the bonds.

▼

Example

At age 45, Gordon had built a sizable portfolio of GICs in his RRSP, but he was not pleased with the recent low rates of return he was earning on these investments. While this fixed income portfolio was only part of his total investment portfolio, he was ready to look for fixed income investment alternatives.

Gordon had just read some material from his financial institution on stripped bonds. He liked the flexibility of being able to buy and sell whenever he wanted; and he liked being able to buy a 20-year bond. This option seemed particularly attractive because when interest rates were high, he could lock them in for a long time — much longer than the five years permitted by GICs. And he really liked the higher returns available on some stripped bonds.

Gordon got a second opinion on stripped bonds from his investment advisor. Gordon decided he would introduce stripped bonds to his GIC portfolio gradually as the GICs matured. He would reinvest in stripped bonds and select a longer maturity date if interest rates were high and a shorter-term bond if interest rates were low. As a conservative investor, Gordon also decided to buy only Government of Canada stripped bonds, to ensure that he owned high-quality investments.

Gordon thought that it would be wise to utilize his financial institution's expertise with stripped bonds to help him understand what to do. So he and the institution set up a game plan to work together on Gordon's portfolio as he added the stripped bonds. The institution suggested that Gordon consider setting up a laddered bond portfolio — that is, purchasing stripped bonds that mature at regular time intervals over a period of years. That way, Gordon would have a bond maturing potentially each year which could be spent or reinvested. Such a portfolio could also prevent him from having all his fixed income investments mature in one year when interest rates were low and reinvestment at these low rates would not be desirable.

STRATEGY #28

Lock In Value and Defer Tax Using Put Options

If you own a stock that has appreciated in value, there is a way to protect that accrued capital gain while holding onto the stock and continuing to defer tax that will be due on this gain when you eventually sell. Buying a stock market *derivative* product called a *put option* can protect your capital gain against future price declines. Acquiring a put option means buying an *option contract* to sell stock at a set price, known as the "*strike price*," during a specific time period.

The fact that it is an option means you can act on the option or not; it's your choice. If you purchase the put option and the price of the stock goes above the strike price, you get the benefit of the increased price on your existing stock less the cost of the put option, which you then let expire unused.

If the stock price declines, you may sell that put option by itself in the market, since the option will increase in value as the stock price declines. Or you can sell your shares at the strike price by exercising the option before it expires. Either way, the sale of the option or the exercise of the option allows you to realize your existing stock gains that accrued before buying the option, and also permits you to further gain in the stock price rise. However, the premium you pay for the option contract must be factored into the total profitability of the transaction.

Put options can be purchased from investment brokerages. Options are sophisticated instruments, and you should seek the advice of a qualified professional advisor if you are inexperienced with buying options on your own.

An additional tip: purchase options that don't expire until next year, in order to defer the potential sale of the stock and the resultant tax on the gain to a future year.

And one final note about put options: they may be available only on a limited number of stocks — likely blue-chip stocks trading on recognized markets around the world.

▼

Example

Duncan bought his shares in West Corp. for $30 per share and the stock is now trading at $40 per share. Duncan believes that the stock price may take a temporary fall but still has long-term value, and he wants to keep his $10-per-share gain without selling the shares. Through his *full-service investment advisor,* Duncan has purchased a put option for $2 per option where the put gives Duncan the right to sell shares of West Corp. at $40 each — until February of next year.

With the put option in place, Duncan can do no worse than his existing $10-per-share gain less the $2-per-option cost of the put option. If the value of the stock decreases below $40, Duncan's option increases in value because he has the right to sell at $40; i.e., any loss in stock value is offset by an increase in option value. If the value of the stock increases beyond $40, Duncan benefits through his share ownership and lets the option expire unused.

Duncan has accomplished his goal of limiting the risk of loss on his shares. In a fairly inexpensive way, he has been able to lock in his existing stock gains. Additionally, because the option doesn't expire until next year, Duncan has also deferred taxation on the eventual sale of the stock or option until the next year.

STRATEGY #29

Buy Assets from Your Spouse

Tax-smart investing can sometimes be achieved very effectively in simple ways. This strategy is a good example. Many families have one spouse earning income that is being taxed in the highest tax bracket, at approximately 50%. The other spouse may have little or no income. Unfortunately, due to the *attribution rules* in the *Income Tax Act*, the higher-earning spouse cannot gift money to the other spouse to invest and have the other spouse pay tax on the investment income at a lower tax rate. Because of these attribution rules, the income earned on the transferred funds is attributed back to the higher-earning spouse and taxed in his or her hands. Nevertheless, when one spouse has a much lower *marginal tax rate*, the desired goal is to move some of the highly taxed investment income of the higher-earning spouse into the hands of the lower-taxed spouse.

A tax-smart investing strategy to accomplish this objective is available when the lower-earning spouse owns some valuable assets, either completely or partially. If, for example, the lower-earning spouse inherited a cottage from his or her parents, or inherited some valuable antiques, or used some of his or her own income to purchase part of the family home or cottage, there may be an opportunity to save tax. The key is that the lower earner must be the property owner; that is, this person inherited the asset or used his or her own funds to buy the asset.

The lower-income spouse could sell this valuable asset (e.g., the cottage) or share of an asset (e.g., half of the family home) to the higher-earning spouse for *fair market value.* Note that any accrued gain on the property sold to the spouse will be taxed (unless the home is a principal residence), and this tax cost should be considered in determining the overall economic benefit of the transaction. Also, in order for the transaction to take place at fair market value for tax purposes, the couple will have to elect out of the automatic transfer at cost between spouses. This transaction will permit the higher-earning spouse to transfer investable wealth (as payment for the asset) to the lower-earning spouse *without* triggering the attribution rules of the Income Tax Act. The lower-earning spouse can then invest the proceeds received from the sale and pay tax on the related investment income at a lower tax rate than the higher-earning spouse would on earning that income. This means that instead of a potential 50% tax rate on the resulting investment, a much smaller tax rate would apply. In fact, there will be no tax at all on the first several thousand dollars of investment income if the lower-earning spouse has no other income. Moreover, the couple will save this amount every year that income continues to be generated on the invested funds and taxed in the lower-earning spouse's hands.

Note, however, that the resulting taxable income in the lower-earning spouse's hands will reduce or eliminate the married exemption tax credit.

▼

Example

Mae earns a salary of $100,000 and investment income of approximately $24,000. She pays tax at a marginal rate of 50%. Her husband, Jim, makes $22,000 a year and has a marginal tax rate of 27%. Jim's last surviving parent passed away recently and Jim inherited the family cottage worth $300,000. In order to take advantage of tax-smart investing, Jim and Mae decided he should immediately sell the cottage to Mae.

Mae verified that the legal costs and land transfer taxes associated with the sale of the cottage were immaterial compared to the tax savings involved. The transaction was formalized by their lawyer and approved by their accountant shortly after. Jim and Mae consulted their tax accountant to ensure that the appropriate tax elections were made such that the attribution rules would not apply to the transaction. Mae sold off some of her non-RRSP investment portfolio in order to buy the cottage, being careful to sell investments that didn't trigger any *taxable capital gains*, by selling some of her *Treasury bills* instead of her stocks. (Mae could have sold her investments directly to Jim in exchange for the cottage.)

Upon receiving the cheque from Mae, Jim invested the proceeds into a balanced investment portfolio consisting of *equity mutual funds, bonds,* and Treasury bills. This transaction shifted approximately $24,000 of annual investment income (historical income, which may not be as high in the future!) into Jim's hands for tax purposes, and will save approximately $3,000 in taxes every year that the money is invested.

Crunching the Numbers

Before the sale: $300,000 worth of investments owned by Mae earning 8% would generate approximately $24,000 of investment income annually. Mae would pay approximately 50% tax on this income and keep only $12,000 after-tax.

After the sale (ignoring non-income tax consequences such

as professional fees and any land transfer taxes): $300,000 worth of investments are now owned by Jim, who has invested them and expects to earn an 8% rate of return annually. Jim will pay approximately 27% in tax on $8,000 and 43% on $16,000 of the investment income, or total tax of $9,040 on the $24,000 of investment income. Jim and the family will now keep $14,960 ($24,000 less $9,040) of income after-tax every year, for an increase of $2,960 annually.

STRATEGY #30

Increase Your RRSP Contribution Room

It is generally in everyone's best interest to pack as much into his or her *RRSP* as possible. Besides contributing as much as possible and as early as possible to your RRSP using your regular contribution room, consider using some other techniques to get money into your RRSP.

Retiring Allowance

An employee leaving an employer due to either retirement or forced early departure may receive a payment for lengthy service called a *retiring allowance.* If the employer agrees to pay a retiring allowance, some or all of the amount may be automatically transferred into the employee's RRSP, tax free, based on eligibility criteria according to the *Income Tax Act.* Employees leaving their employers for one reason or another should consider negotiating their final pay package to include a qualifying retiring allowance. Consult a tax advisor to ensure that any payment received meets the criteria for a retiring allowance that can be transferred to an RRSP.

Increasing RRSP Contribution Room

RRSP contribution room is based on *earned income* in the previous year. Earned income consists primarily of *employment income* and *self-employment income.* Individuals with the ability to control their annual pay (e.g., owners of incorporated businesses) should consider paying themselves enough salary to contribute the maximum to their RRSP each year. To make the maximum contribution of $13,500 in 1998, individuals should pay themselves or negotiate to receive earned income of at least $75,000 ($13,500/18%) in 1997.

▼

Example

Murray owns a successful small company in which he is an active owner/manager. The corporation earns about $400,000 a year before taxes. He recently hired a new tax accountant, who reviewed his company's books for tax-saving opportunities. The accountant noted that Murray and his wife (who also worked in the business) were in the habit of drawing only $50,000 in salary from the business each year. The accountant pointed out that Murray and his wife should consider raising their salaries to at least $75,000 a year in order to be able to contribute the maximum $13,500 each to their RRSPs annually. This strategy could have several advantages for Murray and his wife:

- They would be able to increase the size of their RRSPs much faster and have a more comfortable retirement; this is the key benefit.
- They would receive a larger tax deduction annually by taking advantage of the larger related contribution room and actually contributing more.
- A special low tax rate applies to the first $200,000 of business income of Canadian private companies. Income in

excess of this amount is taxed at regular corporate rates. If the income in excess of $200,000 is kept in the corporation and paid out to shareholders in the form of dividends, some double taxation results (on the income in the company and on the dividend to the individual shareholder). For this reason, advisors often recommend that owner/managers pay out sufficient salary from a corporation to reduce the business earnings to $200,000.

- If their small business needs more cash to operate, Murray and his wife could always lend the money back to the company.

Crunching the Numbers

At their current salary levels of $50,000 each, Murray and his wife can contribute only $9,000 each to their RRSPs annually. But at $75,000 salary levels, they could contribute the maximum $13,500 each year. Assuming there is no change in the maximum contribution amount, and their RRSPs grow at 8% annually compounded, combined additional contributions of $9,000 ([$13,500 – $9,000] x 2) per year would result in additional savings of $411,000 in 20 years.

▼

A Word of Caution

An important point to note about this strategy is that it is more effective when the business is earning more than $200,000 annually and income is taxed at a much higher tax rate in the company than it would be below the $200,000 level. At income levels under $200,000 inside the company, the success of this strategy is more dependent upon significant tax-sheltered growth within the owner/manager's RRSP.

Business owners should consult a professional tax advisor to integrate company and personal tax-planning objectives.

STRATEGY #31

Gift Money to Your Adult Children

If you meet a few criteria, you should consider gifting money to your adult children. (Adult children are children aged 18 or older.) The criteria are as follows:

- You can afford to part with the money permanently, and wish to help out your children with various expenditures in the future;
- You believe that your children have the financial common sense to use the money wisely and also have a need for the money;
- You are not concerned about your children's marital situations or the possibility of their personal *bankruptcy*.

Gifting can have significant tax advantages. If you are in the highest *tax bracket* in Canada and are paying tax at approximately 50%, gifting cash to adult children in lower tax brackets can have several benefits:

- If you use the gift to start an RRSP for your adult children, the RRSP investment eliminates all current tax on the investment (since it is now tax sheltered) and will save all of the tax you would otherwise pay on investment income.
- If the gift is used to pay off a mortgage, your adult children will be able to reduce or eliminate paying non-tax-deductible interest costs out of their disposable income. This means that gifting them $1,000 costs you $30 in interest ($1,000 gift x 6% interest you could have earned x 50% tax rate). On the other hand, the gift saves the children $80 ($1,000 mortgage reduction x 8% mortgage interest rate) they would otherwise be paying on the mortgage. That's a net $50 improvement to the family.
- Even if the adult children just invest the gift, tax will be saved by the family overall if their marginal tax rates are lower than yours.
- The gift can be used to pay for post-secondary education.

▼

Example

Ivy decided she wanted to start her son Billy off right by making the initial contribution to a new RRSP for him. Billy is 20, in university, and (like most students) short on cash, especially to invest. Since age 15, however, Billy had been filing tax returns to report his summer job income, and he had accumulated RRSP contribution room of $4,800.

Ivy made a $4,800 RRSP contribution for Billy in 1997 and by doing so accomplished several *tax-smart* investing goals:

- She reduced the tax she was paying on the investment earnings from 50% to 0% inside Billy's RRSP (although RRSP savings are only a tax deferral).

- She started Billy's RRSP 10 to 20 years earlier than anyone his age might. Due to the power of compounding for the next 60 years, Billy should have a large head start on his retirement plan.
- She made the contribution for Billy but he did not take the tax deduction. Instead, he is saving the tax deduction until after he graduates and has a higher income level. At that time, the deduction can be applied against income that would be taxed in a higher tax bracket, and this will result in a larger tax refund to Billy.

Crunching the Numbers

The RRSP contribution of $4,800, growing at 8% a year and compounded for 60 years, will amount to $486,000. Had Ivy not made the contribution, and Billy had instead made the contribution in 10 years' time when he had sufficient funds, that same amount, growing at 8% a year but compounded for only 50 years, would amount to $225,000. That's a difference of $261,000. Clearly, it pays to start early!

STRATEGY #32

Claim Investment Expenses as Tax Deductions

As part of *tax-smart* investing, you may incur a variety of expenses along the way. It is easy to overlook several tax deductions associated with investing. Here is a list of investment expenses that you can deduct annually on your tax return. Deduct these fees in the year they are paid.

- Safety deposit box charges
- Safe custody expenses
- Accounting expenses for record-keeping of your investments
- Investment management expenses
- Investment counselling expenses

Not all investment management and counselling fees are tax deductible; e.g., fees to consult on an *RRSP portfolio* are not tax deductible. Consult a tax professional to determine which of your fees qualify.

Here are a few more things to note about fees:

- Generally, in order to be tax deductible, fees must be incurred to earn income. This means that the fees being paid are undertaken to result in an income stream. Fees incurred with respect to your RRSP are specifically not tax deductible.
- Many of us pay transaction charges and *loads* every time we buy or sell *stocks, bonds,* or *mutual funds.* Such fees are generally not tax deductible on your personal tax return. Instead, transaction charges for specific purchases are either added to the cost of the related investment or deducted from the proceeds of disposition.

▼

Example

Every year Ted has his accountant prepare his tax return. This involves the tedious task of calculating Ted's gains and losses from his annual investment trading — a task that Ted's accountant does not enjoy. The accountant bills Ted $1,200 for this accounting work every year.

Ted's many trading activities are a result of his monthly discussions with a fee-based investment advisor. Each month Ted gets together with his advisor to discuss investment strategies and market conditions and to review Ted's portfolio. For each meeting Ted is billed $400, but he feels the regular meetings are helping him to invest better.

When Ted and his accountant got together recently to go over Ted's tax return, Ted complained about the high fees for the accounting and also mentioned the cost of his counselling fees. The accountant appreciated Ted's concern and pointed out that the cost should be evaluated on an after-tax basis. Both the investment bookkeeping fees and the counselling fees are tax deductible, meaning that at Ted's tax bracket — the highest — the extra fees are only costing him about half of what he pays upfront, because the other half accounts for tax deduction.

Ted was not used to thinking in "after-tax" terms but agreed with the accountant that after-tax is what is really important. Learning that the fees were tax deductible helped him to understand the true cost of the services.

STRATEGY #33

Don't Get a Tax Refund

If your employer is deducting too much income tax from your pay cheque, it could be costing you a lot of money each year. Each spring, many Canadians look forward to receiving tax-refund cheques after filing their personal tax returns. A refund should be viewed with concern, however, not satisfaction. It means that your source deductions (the income tax withheld on your pay cheque) are all too high. It means that you are losing the benefit of having that extra pay in your pocket all year long; instead, you are loaning it to the government, interest free, until next April. This money, if invested in your name, could be generating income for you throughout the year.

You may be getting a refund because you claimed an *RRSP* deduction, or paid tax-deductible child care or alimony, or made a large charitable contribution. But your employer may not know you're contributing to an RRSP, or paying child care expenses or alimony, or making other selected payments that qualify for a significant deduction on your personal tax return. If your employer is in the dark, the source deductions from your pay cheque are being calculated assuming there are no significant deductions available.

If too much income tax is being withheld, you have lost the opportunity to make money. Here's a way to improve the situation. Investigate whether your employer will send part of your salary directly to your RRSP by payroll deduction, eliminating the need for you to make the *RRSP contribution*. Companies that do this generally don't have to withhold income tax on the amounts so transferred.

Your other option is to mail in a request to the Source Deductions section at your *Revenue Canada* Tax Services Office for a reduction in payroll withholdings. State what you earn. Include proof of your regular RRSP contribution or other qualifying significant annual deductions. Indicate that you expect these deductions to continue into the future. If your request is approved by the government, your employer will receive a letter from Revenue Canada authorizing a reduction in the amount of tax withheld. At this point you should start to notice the increase in your pay cheques!

▼

Example

Every April, Gwen would march around the office announcing how she would spend that year's whopping tax refund. She never thought much about the tax refund's origin — until she did some *tax-smart* planning.

Gwen realized that her annual refund was due to a combination of her RRSP deduction and her alimony deduction from the alimony she pays to her ex-husband. This year Gwen wrote to Revenue Canada explaining why she deserved a withholding-tax reduction: because both deductions should continue into the future, resulting in continued refunds. She provided Revenue Canada with proof of her regular contributions to her RRSP and the future alimony payments she would make.

Revenue Canada agreed and told Gwen's employer to reduce her tax withholdings. Now she gets $55 more each pay cheque (after-tax) and has more cash in her pocket all year long.

Well, sort of. Gwen went one step further and increased her *mortgage* payments by the $55 extra cash. This $55 contribution against the mortgage principal each month allows Gwen to reduce the size of her mortgage faster.

STRATEGY #34

Make Your Interest Expense Tax Deductible

Borrowing as a Tax Strategy

Interest expense is generally tax deductible if the money is borrowed to earn income from a business or property. This excludes investments inside an RRSP, but if you borrow money to purchase a mutual fund outside an RRSP, the interest you pay on the loan will be tax deductible.

To make your interest expense tax deductible, complete the following process. Consider selling some of your existing investments to pay off any non-tax-deductible debt you currently have, and then borrow to reinvest. Be careful not to trigger any substantial capital gains on the sale of the investments. You may have some Canada Savings Bonds or GICs and at the same time be carrying a *line of credit* balance or a vehicle loan. Use the investments to pay off the debts and then borrow again and purchase another investment outside your RRSP. The interest on the newly borrowed funds becomes tax deductible since the borrowed funds are being used to earn investment income on the new investment. Note, however, that if you plan to sell investments with an accrued gain, you will be taxed immediately on any gain you realize.

Don't try to shorten the process above by borrowing money to pay off the debts, leaving the existing investments in place, and then just saying that the new debt was incurred to invest. This will not be acceptable to Revenue Canada. To make the interest expense tax deductible, you should create a paper trail of documentation where you physically sell the existing investments, pay off the current debt, and then reinvest using the new loan proceeds.

Borrowing as an Investment Strategy

If your investment advisor is recommending that you borrow money to invest, and the advisor will earn greater commissions as a result, have him or her justify the reasons for the need to borrow. Take note that *leveraged* investments (investments purchased with borrowed funds) will likely have to earn a consistently higher rate of return than the loan in order to make the borrowing worthwhile. If you plan to borrow to invest, compare the after-tax investment rate of return against the after-tax cost of the interest on the debt. The after-tax investment return must exceed the after-tax interest cost in order for the strategy to be worthwhile. In other words, if the loan interest rate would be 10%, for an individual paying 50% tax, then borrowing to invest would result in a 5% after-tax interest cost. This means that in order for leveraging to be worthwhile, the investment must earn greater than 5% *after-tax* each year the debt is outstanding.

If you borrow to purchase a fixed income investment or preferred shares, the related interest is deductible only up to the amount of income from the investment (for Canadian dividends, up to 1.25 times the dividend). Common shares have the potential to pay any amount of dividends, and therefore the interest should be fully deductible. In addition, capital gains are not considered to be income from property.

Therefore, if your investment has no potential to earn income, but only capital gains, the related interest is not deductible.

So the question is, will you be able to consistently earn a *pre-tax return* exceeding the pre-tax cost of the debt? Achieving a 5% after-tax rate of return year after year may be difficult to do. Using interest income and the same tax bracket, this would require a 10% pre-tax return each year. And if you lose money on your investments purchased with borrowed money, the percentage loss is magnified significantly: you lose part of your original investment, still have to pay interest on a loan, and still have to repay the loan. Remember, you are offsetting a fixed liability with a variable asset!

So if you plan to borrow to invest, be cautious, as profitability is not guaranteed and the whole idea may not be as attractive as it first appears. As a long-term strategy, borrowing to invest can be a profitable undertaking. But when deciding whether to try this strategy, examine a few "what if" scenarios using different possible rates of return with the investments. And get a second opinion from a financial advisor who is qualified to determine if borrowing to invest makes sense for your personal finances.

▼

Example

Phyllis recently found herself incurring more and more interest expense on her monthly credit card bill. She just couldn't get ahead and wanted to do something about it before it got out of control. So Phyllis went to see her financial planner about her predicament. Her financial planner noticed that Phyllis had $5,000 in Canada Savings Bonds she had accumulated for no particular purpose. The planner suggested to Phyllis that she cash in the bonds and pay off her outstanding credit card bill completely. The planner also suggested that Phyllis get into the habit of paying off her credit card bill in full each month in order to avoid incurring high interest charges. The planner also commented that if Phyllis didn't have the money to pay off the credit card, she should consider getting a lower-interest consumer loan from her financial institution and using the proceeds to pay off the credit card bill — in effect, replacing more expensive debt with less expensive debt to improve her cash flow.

Phyllis followed the financial planner's recommendations by cashing in the bonds and paying off the debt. Her credit card company was charging her interest at 15% annually. Since this interest was being paid with after-tax income, at her 50% marginal tax rate the interest expense was costing her 30% in before-tax dollars. Just by paying off this interest expense, she arguably earned a rate of return equal to the difference between 30% and what she had been earning on the investments she sold to pay the debt.

The planner had also recommended that if Phyllis wanted to increase her ability to invest, she should consider borrowing from her financial institution and investing the proceeds in an investment that meets her needs and risk preference. This strategy would make her interest expense tax deductible since the loan proceeds would be used to buy investments that would generate investment income. But in this case, Phyllis decided not to borrow to invest. She didn't need the extra investment income and was more concerned about extinguishing her credit card debt.

▼

Bonus Tips

- Some credit card companies in Canada still charge you interest on the entire balance outstanding on your bill, *after* you make a partial payment. Only when you pay off the entire amount outstanding do the interest charges stop. So try to pay all of the balance due each month.
- Sometimes investors borrow money to invest, lose money on the investment, and are then left with a debt to pay and no investment. Upset with the loss, many investors will make it a priority to pay off this investment debt — but that may not be the *tax-smart* thing to do. Even with the related investment wiped out, the interest expense on the investment loan can continue to be tax deductible. It is wise for an investor to apply free cash flow to non-tax-deductible debt (e.g., a mortgage, credit cards) first, because that interest expense is not tax deductible.
- Beware Revenue Canada's superficial loss rules. These rules prevent a taxpayer or his or her spouse from claiming a loss for tax purposes after selling a losing investment to realize a loss and then repurchasing the same investment. When reinvesting, invest in different securities, or wait at least 30 days to reinvest in order to avoid the superficial loss rules.

STRATEGY #35

Reduce Capital Gains Using Capital Losses

When you invest in *stocks* and *equity mutual funds*, you hope to earn *capital gains*. Because the price you pay for the stocks or equity mutual funds can go up and down on the stock market, you may earn a capital gain or a *capital loss*. A capital gain or loss is the difference between your proceeds on sale and the original cost of the investment. A capital gain will be taxed at approximately 38% for a Canadian in the top marginal tax bracket. That's a lot of gain to lose on the sale!

Here are two strategies to help you minimize that tax. If you plan to sell the investment with the gain near the end of the year, consider waiting until after the final trade date that settles in the same year (there are three business days between trade and settlement date). The gain will then be taxable in the next year, and tax will be due in April of the year after that; a nice deferral of tax for a short period of time. Of course, the tax motive for this strategy becomes secondary if you need the funds from the sale immediately and can't afford to wait to sell, or if investment market conditions warrant an immediate sale.

A second strategy is to sell another stock or equity mutual fund that has an equal-sized capital loss, before the end of the year. For tax purposes, capital gains and capital losses offset one another when they occur in the same calendar year. It is worthwhile to review your non-RRSP investment portfolio before the end of each year. You may have losing investments that it makes sense to sell to reduce your tax bill on the successful investments you sold during the year.

Keep in mind that you shouldn't sell investments with a current accrued loss just to reduce your tax bill. Sell investments you were planning to sell anyway, or sell investments that make sense to sell for the right investment reasons. And if you own investments that are currently in loss positions but you want to hold on to because you think they will rebound, you could still sell the investment, trigger the loss, and repurchase the same investments after 30 days have passed. Note that neither you nor your spouse can repurchase the investment within 30 days before or after the sale of the old investment or else you will be denied access to the capital loss.

▼

Example

Wayne likes to dabble in the stock market and has had a pretty good year so far. As of the end of last month, November, he had capital gains of $14,000 that will be taxable for this year. But Wayne then realized he had two problems. First, he had already reinvested the proceeds from these gains and didn't have the cash available to pay the taxes due on these gains next April. Second, he doesn't like to pay taxes. He was wondering what to do.

Wayne was talking to his neighbour about his investment successes and failures this year. The neighbour told Wayne to consider selling some of his investment "losers" to produce capital losses that would offset the capital gains. Only the net taxable capital gains for the year are taxable. If he could offset the gain completely, he wouldn't have to pay any tax on the gain next April.

Wayne liked this idea and went to his investment advisor to evaluate his investment portfolio. Together, Wayne and the investment advisor evaluated all of Wayne's investments. Some of his loser investments still had promise and the two decided it made sense not to sell them. There were other investments, however, that they believed had no hope of ever producing a gain. In the end, Wayne decided to sell a few investments before December 31, for total capital losses of $8,000.

The losses reduced the net gains for the current year to $6,000 and his taxable capital gain to $4,500. While Wayne still has to pay some tax, he finds this amount much easier to swallow. He realizes that overall he is still better off, since he made money realizing the gains in the first place!

STRATEGY #36

Build Planning into Your Tax Return Preparation

Why is it that individuals seek to pay the least amount of money possible to have their tax returns prepared, yet tax is probably the largest expenditure they will make in their lifetime. Isn't good tax planning worth paying for?

The world of Canadian income taxes is complex, confusing, and always changing. In 1997 alone there were dozens of new pages added to the *Income Tax Act.* Professional tax accountants spend all year long understanding new tax rules and how to use the rules effectively for their clients.

If you do not work with income tax every day, it is difficult to stay on top of all the changes. Failure to take advantage of a *tax deduction* or *tax credit* could result in an inflated tax bill every year as long as you live, and could potentially cost you thousands of dollars during your lifetime.

This strategy is aimed at individuals who complete their own personal tax return every year. While this strategy applauds your hard work, it suggests that you get a little help now and then to ensure that you remain on the right track. A review of the accuracy of your return by a tax specialist and a review for planning opportunities can help to ensure that you are taking advantage of all credits and deductions you are entitled to — today, and as your life changes. It will also determine if there are extra steps you and your family can take to minimize and defer tax.

A qualified tax specialist is not someone who simply prepares tax returns. A qualified tax specialist is an individual trained in the laws of the Income Tax Act of Canada and capable of understanding how the rules can be used to save you tax. It is *tax planning*, not *tax compliance* (return preparation), that can result in tax savings and deferral. Tax planning is where the value is, and is worth a lot more than the mechanical process of completing a return. If you are simply preparing your tax return each year, you may not be doing any tax planning at all!

Consider having a qualified specialist review your tax return every three years. Three years because that is as far back as a taxpayer can normally refile to correct errors or omissions found in the return. If a tax specialist only reviews it, but you still complete it, the cost of hiring the tax professional should be lower. Ask the specialist for tax-planning ideas related to your family, your job, investing, and your estate, as part of the return review. One good strategy could pay for this review over and over again. And if you currently have a tax accountant, consider getting a second opinion from another — just as you would with a doctor.

▼

Example

Susie proudly boasts that she does her own tax return each April, and has done it for the last 15 years. But this year she decided to have a friend who is a C.A. review her 1997 tax return, because she heard there were some significant changes to the Income Tax Act in the last few years and maybe they have affected her. She left the return with him, and after a week they got together to discuss his review. He had some suggestions. Here are two:

- Susie and her husband, Michael, were each claiming their own charitable donations on their respective tax returns. Each was claiming about $200. The accountant told Susie to claim all the donations on one return, since the tax rules provide a higher tax credit on donations in excess of $200 each year. By claiming all the donations on one return, Susie and Michael could increase their federal tax credit from 17% to 29%, because total donations made by an individual that are greater than $200 are credited at a higher rate. This would save them more tax every year.
- Susie and Michael had incurred some substantial medical fees last year due to a medical condition Michael developed. These expenses amounted to $20,000 and hadn't been claimed by Susie when doing their tax returns. The accountant explained that these expenses did qualify as a tax credit and would reduce their tax bill by several thousand dollars this year.

Susie was shocked about the charitable donations tip, as she told the accountant they'd done this for ten years. The C.A. added that they could go back three years to file adjustments that should generate refunds from the changes they would make. Susie was doubly grateful for the medical expense tip, as this would result in significant additional savings. The $300 visit to the accountant was more than paid for!

STRATEGY #37

Save Tax by Starting a Part-Time Business

As an employee, you have limited opportunities to save tax related to your *employment income,* other than maximizing your RRSP contributions. Self-employed individuals, however, can deduct expenses incurred to earn their business income, which will help to reduce their taxable income. Examples of expenditures that may qualify include vehicle operating costs, parking, telephone charges, stationery, office supplies, faxes, costs associated with a home office including rent, interest and depreciation, utilities, professional fees, meals and entertainment, and many other types of costs if they are related to earning the business income.

Individuals often turn part-time hobbies into profitable businesses. The key word here is profitable: in order for Revenue Canada to accept your business deductions, the business must reasonably have the ability to be profitable.

If you are considering starting a business, it is advisable to consult a tax accountant on setting up your accounting books, employing family members, what to deduct for tax, *GST* and PST or HST issues, business taxes, whether to incorporate or not, use of a home office, and the many other issues related to starting a business. Many financial institutions are now also focusing on small-business owners and can be a valuable source of information about starting a small business.

▼

Example

Cathy was enjoying her analyst job with the local municipal government; a seven-hour day and no weekend work was resulting in more personal time, but she was also feeling the pinch with the smaller salary for the shorter hours. With all her spare time, Cathy decided to use her accounting background to open a home-based bookkeeping business.

Cathy used her personal network to quickly acquire four clients. She then visited her lawyer to talk about the right business structure. They agreed the business was too small and simple to bother incorporating yet, and Cathy wasn't too concerned about the legal liability associated with unincorporated businesses. Cathy could run the business as an unincorporated *sole proprietorship*. That means Cathy could simply report her revenues and expenses on her personal tax return each year.

Next, Cathy went to her financial institution. She opened a new account for the business and also applied for a credit card for the business. She knew the importance of keeping the business expenses separated from her personal ones. Also, the credit card statement would serve as a nice monthly expense summary. Both of these steps would help to simplify the business accounting and provide a nice audit trail of her business revenues and expenses should Revenue Canada ever come calling.

Cathy used some of her savings to purchase a computer and some accounting and word-processing software. She bought some office supplies and furniture and set up an office in her home. Before long, Cathy had the business up and running, working a few hours a week. At her current work load, she anticipated her year's gross revenues would be $10,000.

From a tax point of view, Cathy was confident she was going to have a profitable business. Because expected revenues would be less than $30,000, she wouldn't bother to register for the Goods and Services Tax (GST), which was her choice at this sales level. Instead, she would eliminate an administrative hassle. This meant, however, that she would lose the ability to recover GST paid — a trade-off that she had already evaluated.

With a home office to work out of and meet clients in, Cathy is planning to write off a portion of the *mortgage* interest, utility costs, home insurance, repairs and maintenance, and other home costs, based on the office square footage as a percentage of her total home square footage.

Since Cathy doesn't plan to use her car for her business, she doesn't have to worry about keeping a logbook and tracking vehicle expenses. Other costs she may be able to write off could include office supplies, phone calls for business including rental charges, software costs, advertising, half the cost of business meals and entertainment, and *depreciation*. Depreciation (also called capital cost allowance for tax purposes) represents the write-off of the cost of business assets, such as the computer hardware and her desk, over their useful lives. Depreciation is not a simple deduction, however, and additional tax may result on the eventual sale of the asset being depreciated.

STRATEGY #38

Beware Offshore Tax Havens for the Average Canadian

For most of us, the idea of placing money offshore, out of the hands of Revenue Canada, is a pleasant dream. In reality, there are few opportunities for the average Canadian to defer or eliminate tax using a legitimate *offshore trust* strategy.

Canadian residents are taxable on their worldwide income. This means that as long as you live in Canada, you are generally required to report all income earned anywhere in the world, regardless of how or where, on your Canadian tax return. This generally includes income in an offshore trust where Canadian residents have an interest in that trust. There are some exceptions, however, to this general rule in the context of offshore trusts. If the trust is established by a non-resident settlor — the contributor of the property in the trust — and has a non-resident trustee, the undistributed income will not be subject to Canadian tax if the settlor is a resident of Canada for less than 60 months. Income distributed to a Canadian beneficiary will be taxable. This exception is particularly useful in the context of the multinational family where different family members are resident in different jurisdictions and there is a genuine intention by the non-residents to benefit the Canadian residents.

Without getting into a lot of detail, this is what to remember: if you are a conservative Canadian with average wealth, you plan to always live in Canada, and your relatives are Canadian and will likely always live in Canada, there are generally no opportunities to save tax on investments using a legitimate offshore strategy. However, if you are ever planning to leave Canada permanently, if you have relatives who are not Canadian and want to become Canadian, or if these non-Canadian relatives want to leave you family assets from their estate, then you should consider consulting a qualified tax advisor about offshore tax strategies.

For individuals in Canada who believe that placing money in an offshore bank account and not reporting income on your Canadian tax return is an acceptable offshore strategy, be warned that your strategy is against the law. Since you are taxed on your worldwide income as a Canadian resident, you are obliged to report all of your income. If you choose not to report any offshore income, you are committing tax evasion and may face fines and imprisonment for these actions.

Where it is possible, planning the use of offshore trusts should be very carefully structured and paperwork should be precisely prepared. Properly done, this is legitimate tax planning and is not a form of tax evasion. Due to the complexity of this type of planning, ensure that you deal with a global tax advisory service that can deal with the cross-border international issues.

▼

Example

Mitch was an executive and liked to be aggressive with his income taxes. He prepared his own tax return and was always looking for new ways to minimize income taxes paid to Revenue Canada. He was always reading about opportunities to invest outside of Canada, avoiding Canadian tax, and he finally decided to try one.

Mitch applied to open an account with a financial institution in the country of NoTax. He saw the ad in a local newspaper, and while he had never heard of the company, he decided to proceed without any additional research. He filled out the application and sent off the cheque. That was three years ago. Since then, Mitch has never reported the income he has earned from the offshore investment, and he thinks he has created the ideal offshore tax shelter.

Mitch's best friend, Fred, is a tax accountant. Mitch and Fred are close, but up to now they have separated their social and business relationships, and Fred has never given Mitch any tax advice. With Revenue Canada's recent proposed changes requiring Canadians to report certain investments outside of Canada (a law that never existed before), Fred thought he should point this out to Mitch.

Mitch appreciated the information, but stated that it didn't affect him. He said he had money invested far away, beyond the reach of Revenue Canada. Fred looked at Mitch with alarm and stated that wherever Mitch's money was, it might not be beyond the government's reach. Revenue Canada taxes Canadians on their worldwide income, and it is the duty of all Canadians to report all their worldwide income on their tax returns each year, or potentially face penalties if Revenue Canada ever finds out they aren't.

Mitch turned white. While he had enjoyed minimizing income taxes paid by investing outside of Canada, he had always wanted to do it within the realm of Canadian law. He told Fred his entire story, and asked what to do. Fred said that he would help, and that they should refile Mitch's tax returns for the last three years to reflect the unreported income. Mitch may have to pay penalties and interest on the late payment of taxes, but since Mitch will be voluntarily telling all, it may be possible to ask for the penalties to be waived (not the interest).

STRATEGY #39

Protect Your Cottage and Your Business Using Insurance

On death, your cottage, your business, and all other assets owned are deemed to be disposed of for *fair market value.* This means that if the properties were purchased long ago at low cost but have greatly increased in value, the tax bill on death could be significant. So how does the *estate* pay the tax bill due on the final tax return of the deceased individual?

A large tax bill to an estate with few liquid assets could mean that the cottage itself or the family business interest has to be sold to non-family members in order to come up with the cash to pay the tax bill. Very often, family members do not want to sell a cottage that has been in the family for 50 years, or a family business that was supposed to be the future livelihood for the grandchildren. But sadly, the sale of the cottage or business may be the only choice for an estate with few other cash resources to pay the deceased's final tax bill.

These are two situations where purchasing *life insurance* to offset the tax liability on death can make a lot of sense. The policy will pay a tax-free benefit on death which can be used to clear up a large final tax bill arising from a *deemed disposition* of a cottage or business interest.

If ownership of a cottage or business interest will likely be transferred to a surviving spouse on death, the insurance policy should pay out on the death of the second spouse. Because asset transfers between spouses occur at cost, there is no immediate tax on the death of the first spouse. This type of insurance policy is called "joint and last to die." The insurance premiums may also be lower in this case, since the payout will not occur until the death of the last survivor.

▼

Example

Iris and her husband, Frank, have owned their family cottage since before their children were born. They purchased the cottage for $20,000, and it is now worth $320,000. Their children are now over age 30. Iris and Frank are planning to leave the cottage to pass on to their heirs.

Iris knows that on the death of the last surviving spouse, there will be a tax bill of approximately $120,000 to be paid out of their estate before the cottage can be passed on to their children. Iris has been pro-active in taking steps to preserve the cottage in the family, but she is concerned about the taxes that may be due on their death.

The entire family has grown up at the cottage, and no one wants to see it sold. To prevent this, Iris wants to purchase a life insurance policy that will pay the tax bill on death with the tax-free proceeds from the insurance policy. Iris has decided that she and Frank can afford to pay into a life insurance policy over the next 10 years. This cost will affect her cash flow during this 10-year period, but not too badly, and she will achieve a long-term objective that is very important to her and the entire family.

To implement their goal, Iris and Frank have scheduled

meetings with three insurance agents, who will each propose a recommended solution and cost. Iris is also going to ask her financial planner (who is qualified to consult on life insurance) to sit in on the meetings and provide an objective opinion of the agents' products. Iris has never fully understood the "lingo" of life insurance agents, and she thinks that having the financial planner along to help her ask the right questions and compare the presentations makes good sense.

STRATEGY #40

Invest in an RRSP Before You Invest in a Home

Here's your chance to go against the crowd: invest in a home at age 30 and an RRSP at age 20.

This strategy is the reverse of what many people do. People in their 20s typically get a job, get married, maybe buy a home, and have kids. They commit to a 15- to 25-year home *mortgage* which absorbs a lot of their cash flows during that period. During those 15 or more years, RRSP contributions may be made but are generally not maximized because it's hard to find all the necessary cash when there are so many other bills to pay.

Before they know it, people are in their 40s and the mortgage is nearly gone. It's finally time to turn their efforts toward their RRSPs, since retirement may be less than 20 years away. People may also realize at this time that they likely need at least $2 million in capital to live the retirement lifestyle they want, but have only 20 years left to accumulate this amount. In the end, they may not have $2 million when they retire, but they'll have a big, paid-off house!

Suppose instead that an individual in his 20s gets a job,

rents inexpensively or lives at home, and maximizes his RRSP contributions throughout his 20s, before getting married, having kids, and buying a home. In that period of time, the individual can build an RRSP with more than $50,000 in it, depending on his income, spending habits, and other factors.

Then, at age 30, he can purchase a home, and it too may be paid off in 15 to 25 years, although the payments will extend a little later in life due to the late start. Even if his RRSP contributions stop for 15 years, the value of the existing plan may grow to more than $200,000 in that period because of the tax-free compounding. When the individual is in his mid-40s, the mortgage is paid off and he can now continue to build on an already sizable RRSP.

The lesson to be learned here is that the power of compounding money is king. The longer your RRSP is in existence, the larger it will become with little effort or additional money from you. Given this fact, why not start your RRSP as early in life as possible? In addition to letting you build a larger RRSP, buying a home later in life will give you time to build up a larger initial down payment, and your earnings will likely be higher, permitting you to afford larger mortgage payments and reduce your mortgage faster.

One final word about real estate: this strategy assumes that real estate prices rise slowly. This strategy may not be the preferred route when it's possible to buy a home and take advantage of a rapidly rising real estate market.

▼

Example

Robert graduated from university at age 22 and took a job as a programmer with a growing computer company. The job paid $40,000 yearly and Robert immediately opened an RRSP and started making annual contributions of $7,000.

The investments grew at an 8% rate each year. By the time Robert got married to Diane at age 29, he had $58,000 inside his RRSP.

Robert and Diane bought a home that same year and selected a 15-year mortgage amortization period. They had managed to put down 10% toward the purchase. They also planned to apply any future income tax refunds as additional lump-sum payments toward the mortgage in order to pay it down faster. For the next 18 years, Robert and Diane focused on meeting the costs of raising a family. Robert continued to make RRSP contributions, but they averaged only $4,000 a year during that time.

Now, at age 47, Robert has almost finished paying off his mortgage and is maximizing his RRSP contributions easily because of his larger salary and low debt. Based on his contributions and a growth rate of 8%, Robert's RRSP is currently worth $370,000 — even after his relatively small contributions over the last 18 years!

Robert was visiting his neighbour Emil last week. Emil is Robert's age, and the two have always compared their personal finances. Emil was quick to brag that he and his wife had paid off their home five years ago already and had no debt. They had a lot more money to spend on vacations, on the kids, and for investing purposes.

Robert listened quietly and then asked Emil about RRSPs. Had he been able to maximize his contributions, and how much had they been able to save? "We spent most of our spare money on the mortgage in our early years together," Emil said. "Then the kids came, so we didn't really start building our RRSPs until our mid-30s. Today our plans total about $200,000."

Robert smiled. He knew that his mortgage would also be paid off shortly but the early start on his RRSPs has resulted in a plan almost double the size of his neighbour's.

STRATEGY #41

Beware Informal In-Trust Accounts for Children's Savings

Many financial advisors are advising parents to set up a mutual fund account earning capital gains "in trust" for their children, as a savings vehicle for the children. Under the Income Tax Act's *attribution rules,* capital gains earned by a child under age 18 are taxable in the child's hands, not those of the parents who provided the funds for the investment. While this plan appears to produce effective family income-splitting by taxing the capital gains in the child's hands, it may not be that easy. There is a risk that the "in-trust" account will fail to meet Revenue Canada's standards, resulting in the parents being re-assessed and having to pay tax on the capital gains earned in the trust account. Note that a parent, as contributor, will already have to pay tax on any interest or dividends earned.

The first critical question is, does the in-trust account actually form a trust for tax purposes? To qualify, there must be clear identification of the *trustee,* the trust contributor or settlor, and the *beneficiaries.* If the account is titled "Mrs. X in trust for Tommy" and the funds are contributed by Mr. X, the test should be met. It is clear that the mother is the trustee and the child is the beneficiary. Mr. X is the settlor. But an account opened as "Mrs. X in trust" doesn't meet the Revenue Canada test, because the beneficiaries are not named.

Second, has a transfer of funds or investments to the trust actually occurred? Revenue Canada says the settlor or trust contributor cannot also be the trustee. So Mr. and Mrs. X should agree that one spouse will provide the funding to the trust and the other spouse will be the trustee. The trustee is solely responsible for the ongoing operation of the trust and the investment decision-making inside the trust. The contributor parent must give up all control of the transferred funds, so that funds or assets cannot revert back to the contributing parent.

Take note: should Revenue Canada decide to declare an in-trust account not to be a valid trust, all of the capital gains from such an account would be taxable back to the contributor.

With an *informal trust,* other concerns may include issues like divorce of the parents, sudden death of the parents, and *bankruptcy* of the parents. How would your informal trust be affected by these situations? And remember, with an informal trust, the children have access to all of the funds inside the trust upon reaching age 18. Are you comfortable with that? So what can be done?

All of the above concerns relating to informal trusts can be averted by putting the trust arrangement in writing and creating a *formal trust.* Consider getting the assistance of a lawyer or accountant with trust experience to establish a formal trust, to explain the pros and cons of a formal trust, and to outline the fees for establishing and maintaining a formal trust. In the end, you may see the decision of whether to create a formal trust as a cost/risk analysis. If the trust arrangement may have significant value down the road, there may be a greater desire to use a formal trust.

▼

Example

Herb and Sara just had a baby and have decided they want to start an education fund for little Zack. Together they visited their local financial institution and asked about setting up an in-trust account for Zack. The customer service representative explained that the institution offered such an account, and proceeded to tell Herb and Sara the important characteristics of the account: the need for one parent to be the contributor and the other the trustee of the trust account; the fact that Zack would have access to the money at age 18; and the desirability of investing the proceeds in an investment producing capital gains in order to shift taxation of the capital gains to Zack (likely resulting in no taxation if Zack has no other income).

Herb and Sara, after talking to their tax advisor, and understanding the details and risk of this type of account, completed an informal trust document prepared by the institution. They also agreed to purchase the institution's blue-chip equity mutual fund with the contributor's investment proceeds. They decided that Sara would contribute toward the account and Herb would be responsible for management. At this point they didn't know if they should consider a formal trust, but decided to revisit the issue in a few years, when they hope to have a better idea of how much money they will save for Zack. A formal trust seemed to make sense only for a more significant amount of money than they had invested right now.

STRATEGY #42

Strategize with Employee Stock Options

Stock options are financial instruments provided by employers that give employees the right to purchase company *shares* at a specified price (*exercise price*) within a specified time period. When the options are *exercised*, the employee pays the exercise price in exchange for the shares, which generally are worth more than the exercise price. From a tax perspective, the difference between the exercise price and the market price of the shares at the time of exercise is taxed as *employment income* in the year the employee exercises the option, unless the company is a *Canadian controlled private corporation* (CCPC), in which case the employee won't be taxed until he or she disposes of the shares. In either case, the employee may be entitled to a stock option deduction on his or her tax return equal to 25% of the amount included in income, if certain conditions are met.

Stock options are a popular form of compensation because the amount of money an employee may eventually receive is tied to the success of the company as measured by share price increases. Thus, a stock option can be a good incentive for employees to chip in to produce a successful company. Many corporations, therefore, like to see employees hold their stock options for the long term, and the companies apply staged vesting periods directing the minimum holding period before the options can be exchanged for shares. This corporate expectation may, however, conflict with some employees' desire for a balanced investment strategy.

Many senior executives may hold significant amounts of options and company shares, which may create excessively risky portfolios since these executives' portfolios may not be well diversified. If the company stock takes a nosedive, so potentially does a significant part of the executives' life savings.

Stock Options and Investment Strategy

The value of stock options and company stock should be included in the determination of a balanced investment portfolio. If the company is a small private company, the company's options and stock should likely be considered as a higher-risk equity component of the portfolio. If the company is a *blue-chip* public corporation, the options may be considered less risky. Discuss the appropriate risk level of your company with a financial advisor. Overall, the company's options and stock should not make up an overwhelming portion of a portfolio, but rather should comprise a portion of the portfolio that meets your *risk tolerance* and *asset mix* expectations. This may require you to exercise some of the options, sell the stock, and re-invest in a more balanced investment selection in order to achieve this balance.

Stock Options and Tax Strategy

Any stock you own that has a large *accrued capital gain* will be taxed when the stock is sold and the gain is realized. Stock options, which may also contain accrued value, will be taxed when the shares that resulted from the option exercise for a private company are sold, or will be taxed when the options for a public company are exercised *and* possibly also when the resulting shares are sold. Strictly from a tax point of view, it is in an employee's best interest to hold existing stock indefinitely and to exercise options at the last possible moment in order to defer taxation. While no tax reductions may be achieved, this strategy will create a *deferral of tax* — perhaps the next best thing. But keep in mind that owning substantial options and shares of any one company may be risky due to a lack of investment diversification.

Stock owned by an employee should be gifted to his or her spouse prior to any further stock option exercise, in order to avoid an *averaging of the cost base* of all the shares. An averaging of the cost base would result in an acceleration of tax payable, since the existing shares likely have an actual cost that is lower than the cost of the new shares. Moving the older shares, which hold a larger accrued gain, to a spouse may permit the employee to sell the newer shares and pay tax currently on a smaller capital gain. The transfer of the other shares to the spouse does not attract immediate taxation because transfers between spouses are deemed to take place at cost. Note, however, that any income and capital gains from the shares gifted to the spouse will still be taxed in the employee's hands.

Share owners of Canadian controlled private companies have an additional option unavailable to public company share owners. Shareholders of private Canadian companies can use a $500,000 capital gains exemption available to every Canadian taxpayer to offset capital gains incurred on the disposal of CCPC shares. Accessing the exemption is not guaranteed, and the criteria should be reviewed with a qualified tax professional. Nevertheless, shareholders of qualifying corporations should make every attempt to take advantage of this exemption.

Overall, What to Do

Selecting a strategy to provide you with financial peace of mind requires you to balance your preference for tax deferral with your investment risk tolerance, while considering your cash-flow needs and any corporate expectations for you to hold options or own company stock. Does this sound like a juggling act? The following points are worth considering.

The first priority is to develop a balanced investment portfolio. Taking steps to protect your retirement nest egg is arguably more important than paying some tax today. This may mean reducing your holdings of options and stock. This can be completed with a lump-sum exercise, stock sale, and reinvestment into other investments, or with a once-a-year exercise-and-sell strategy that produces a more gradual move toward a balanced portfolio. One attractive approach is a series of exercise-and-sell strategies where you can buy other investments over a period of time, hopefully avoiding buying at a market high. Buying over time is a common purchase strategy which reduces risk of any significant losses compared to buying all at once. This series of exercise-and-sell strategies is attractive because employees can continue to share in the success of their companies during the period of exercise. In any case, the options typically expire at specific future dates, so it is important to keep these dates in mind so that you don't forgo any benefits. Employees who are retiring and will no longer be responsible for the success of the company may prefer to sell all their holdings before they retire.

A series of exercise-and-sell strategies can be attractive from a company's point of view also, since the company may prefer this to an all-out dumping of its options and stock. A large sales volume might be perceived negatively by other shareholders and could hurt share price where such transactions are published in newspapers. Selling over a period of time can be more politically friendly and less likely to be noticed publicly. Another drawback to exercising and selling all at once is the high level of taxation that would occur.

The second consideration is taxation. An employee should take steps to utilize the $500,000 capital gains exemption if the shares resulting from the exercised options are for a private qualifying company. A strategy of exercising and selling over time permits the employee to continue to defer some taxation to a later date. As mentioned above, however, existing shareholdings should be gifted to a spouse (or transferred to a holding corporation) before any exercising, in order to minimize and defer tax.

Stocks options and company stock can be a significant portion of an employee's investment portfolio. It is in your best interest to consult a professional advisor who understands all the issues rather than just exercising and selling on your own.

▼

Example

Roberta is a senior vice president with a large public company in Canada. Her RRSP totals $200,000 and consists mostly of company stock, currently valued at $150,000, which has greatly appreciated over the last five years. Roberta also has several thousand company stock options which can be exercised each year for the next five years, and she owns a small amount of stock outside her RRSP.

Roberta's corporation likes to have its executives own corporate shares but does not force the employees to own large amounts. Roberta was uncomfortable with having so much of her RRSP portfolio invested in only one stock investment. She was also unfamiliar with the tax rules for stock options, and wanted to develop a strategy to deal with any tax concerns. After consulting her *financial planner* and a tax accountant experienced with stock option strategies, Roberta decided on the following plan:

1. She would sell 75% of the company stock in her RRSP and invest the proceeds in a combination of government *stripped bonds*, *equity mutual funds*, and *Treasury bills*, based on an *asset allocation* assessment completed by her financial planner. She would sell in four instalments over two years, which would permit her to continue to share in the anticipated company stock price increase expected in the next year. Roberta was confident of this share price increase, based on her experiences in the company and corporate plans for the next year.

   There would be no tax issues for this stock sale since the investments are held inside Roberta's RRSP.
2. She would transfer the non-RRSP stock to her husband, Ali, in order to avoid the averaging of her cost base between these shares and her newly exercised shares discussed below. For tax purposes, these existing shares could be transferred to Ali at cost. This would serve to minimize taxes paid, by permitting her to realize the smaller capital gains on the sale of the newer stock holdings rather than the larger gains from the averaging of cost with the older stock holdings now in her husband's name.
3. Roberta's tax accountant pointed out that Roberta would have to pay tax on any dividend income and future capital gains earned on the shares gifted to Ali.
4. Finally, Roberta would set up a plan to exercise 20% of her options and sell the shares each year for the next five years. Proceeds from the sales would be added to her RRSP, build her non-RRSP savings, and contribute to her child's savings. Roberta realized that tax would be due on these exercises and sales, but accepted this as the trade-off for a balanced investment portfolio.

STRATEGY #43

Consider Universal Life Insurance as an Investment

Some *life insurance* products are becoming increasingly attractive as investment options, in addition to playing an important role in risk management. This strategy focuses solely on this investment component, which can be beneficial in the right situation.

A *universal life insurance* policy is a form of permanent insurance where the insurance component and the savings element are separate and distinct, and the policy owners may have several investment options to consider for the savings piece of the policy, along with flexibility on the timing and amount of premium deposits. The investment options for the savings component can include fixed income instruments, *GICs*, and equity-associated investments. These equity-associated investments can include products tied to the *performance* of the TSE 300, the S&P 500 in the U.S., and other internationally recognized indices. Policy owners do not purchase investments in these indices or their holdings; rather, the life insurance company agrees to pay a comparable rate of return to the change in the index (or indices) in question. Policies may have several investment options which can be varied according to a client's wishes (within the same insurance company). Selection of the type(s) of investments for the savings component of the policy should be made after careful consideration of your *risk/return* preferences and balanced with your total investment portfolio mix.

A universal life insurance policy can provide tax sheltering of death benefits paid out on the policy holder's death, if the policy qualifies as an exempt policy under the *Income Tax Act.* These death benefits will include the accumulations from the savings component of the policy, which can grow tax free inside the policy over the life of the policy. The investment accumulation inside a universal life policy is usually added to the original death benefit amount. If, however, the accumulated savings inside the policy are ever "cashed in" or borrowed against during the life of the policy holder, a taxable transaction can result.

Aside from tax, if you name an individual beneficiary of the policy, the proceeds of the insurance on death pass outside your estate and eliminate the need to pay *probate fees* on the proceeds. There may also be creditor-proofing opportunities associated with owning universal life insurance that are not available with non–life insurance company products.

So what should you be concerned with? For tax reasons, you should try to avoid cashing in the policy before death. That aside, when you are investigating universal life policies, factors to evaluate include the following:

- The number of investment options for the savings component of the policy. Consider a policy with options in a variety of *asset classes.*
- The company's rules and any fees for switching between different investments as your needs and *risk tolerance* change over time.
- The quality of the life insurance company. Purchasing a

universal policy may be a 50-year commitment, and you want the insurance company to be there in 50 years.

- The life insurance company's administration expenses, mortality costs, and other expenses. These costs may affect the success of your investment component if they are factored into the costs of the policy. The treatment of these and other costs may vary by company.
- Accountability of the insurance company. Will it provide minimum credits to the investment funds you select to invest in? The size of credits can be affected by the variables described in the previous point.
- The basis on which the insurance company pays bonuses into the investment component.

In addition to pure insurance objectives, universal life insurance can play a role in your estate plan and investment plan. Given the variety of uses, the wide selection of products available, and the tax and investment complications, careful evaluation of options should be made before purchasing. Consider seeking a second opinion from an accountant or advisor who has expertise with insurance products and can provide independent advice. Have a clear objective in mind when buying, and most importantly, ensure that the policy is affordable to you. There is no sense in buying a policy that rewards death, while the cost of the *premiums* hurt your lifestyle today.

▼

Example

Laurel, a senior executive, is looking for opportunities to reduce and/or tax-shelter some of her income and investments. She is 48, earns $150,000 annually, and is married with 20-year-old twins. She has ample excess cash flow between herself and her husband, Doug, who is a doctor. Recently, her financial advisor introduced her to universal life insurance.

Laurel seems a good candidate for universal life insurance for investment purposes. She has excess cash flow and can afford the cost of the premiums over the next 20 years while she and her husband continue to work. Laurel and Doug are already maximizing their RRSPs, and universal life insurance seems like a good next step for tax sheltering of investment income. Laurel and Doug also want to leave their children a fixed amount when they die. Although Laurel and Doug have the capacity to provide their children with significant funds, they want to keep their RRSPs and their investments for themselves to spend in their retirement, and they are not going to worry about how much of these amounts will be left for the kids. Instead, they would like to purchase an insurance policy that will provide the desired amount for the children — pay for the policy now and be done with it.

Before making the purchase decision, Laurel and Doug listened to several presentations and reviewed several scenario charts provided by their financial advisor. The advisor also provided examples of products from different life insurance companies, the pros and cons of each, and the costs of each. Laurel and Doug found all this data a bit overwhelming, so they enlisted their accountant to help objectively analyze the data and the strategy in general. Their accountant was experienced with life insurance products. The financial advisor, the accountant, and Laurel and Doug together concluded that universal life insurance was affordable and appeared to be a good fit for Laurel and Doug's particular needs. They decided to buy two smaller policies from different institutions in order to split the risk of going with just one company.

Laurel and Doug have scheduled the next meeting with their financial advisor to decide on what investments to purchase in the savings component of the policy. The advisor will help them develop a fit with their overall investment portfolio, after careful consideration of their risk tolerance, their other investments, and their expectations.

STRATEGY #44

Expand RRSP Foreign Content Beyond 20%

Inside your *RRSP*, only 20% of the total cost of your investments can be in investments outside of Canada. With more than 90% of the world's economic activity and investment opportunities occurring outside of Canada, one might say that investing 80% of your life savings in a single, small corner of the world is risky. A widely diversified investment mix is an effective way to manage the risk of loss in your RRSP *portfolio*. Owning investments in many countries is a form of *diversification*, which can reduce the adverse impact on your portfolio return if one of those countries has a bad year.

One way to invest beyond the 20% limit in your RRSP is to purchase *synthetic index mutual funds*. A synthetic index fund replaces actual stock ownership inside an *index* fund with ownership of *futures* contracts that lock in the future change in a particular index. The *fund manager* invests much of the fund's money in Canadian *money market instruments* and uses the rest of the money to buy futures contracts on investments in foreign equity market indices like the S&P 500 in the United States or the Nikkei index in Japan. Futures are *derivatives*, and permit money managers to invest in the rise of an index without actually buying the stocks of an index. Because the cost of futures contracts is just a fraction of the cost of the underlying securities, synthetic index fund managers can buy large amounts of futures representing international investment exposure potentially far in excess of the permitted 20%.

Synthetic index funds should mirror the performance of the stock market indices they are designed to replicate. Stock market indices can represent the combined market value of many of the largest companies in a country, so as an investor purchasing a country's leading index, you may be able to diversify across an entire economy without the risks and additional costs of picking specific companies to invest in.

To learn about investing in index funds outside an RRSP, refer to Strategy #6.

▼

Example

Denise was reviewing her RRSP and was concerned about the large amount of Canadian content inside her plan. While the recent performance of the RRSP investments has been good, she felt uncomfortable that so much of her money was invested in one small country — Canada. Denise called her investment advisor, Diego, to see if there was anything she could do.

Over lunch, Diego educated Denise about the options available to increase the foreign content in her RRSP. Diego pointed out the following strategies:

- The 20% foreign cost limit inside her RRSP is based on original cost, but an increase in the market value of the foreign content will provide additional foreign exposure while cost remains within the 20% rule.

- In Canadian equity mutual funds, many of the corporations invested in by the funds are large multinational corporations that do business around the globe. Since these corporations operate worldwide, their business is diversified and less susceptible to economic downturns in any one country. In effect, the investor is also invested globally, by owning these companies through the mutual fund.
- A Canadian mutual fund that is considered to be 100% Canadian for purposes of the foreign content rules may invest 20% of its holdings in non-Canadian investments. This means that Denise's 80% Canadian content may also have 20% foreign content. Thus, in total, she may have 20% foreign mutual funds plus another 16% (80% x 20%) foreign content inside her Canadian funds, for a total of 36% foreign content.

Diego summarized by noting that a regular Canadian fund may provide good exposure to non-Canadian investments but this may not be apparent without exploring the composition of the fund. A financial advisor can assist with this.

For additional exposure, Denise could consider purchasing index mutual funds that buy futures representing indices of other countries. Diego cautioned that whenever individuals invest outside of Canada, they may face gains or losses on currency from a rise or drop in the value of the Canadian dollar against the foreign currency they are investing in. This means that a gain earned from the rise of the Nikkei Index in Japan may be completely offset by a loss in currency value against the Japanese Yen. Overall, because of currency fluctuations they may have no gain at all! Fluctuations in currency values arise from the impact of a variety of economic and political factors around the world.

Diego further explained that Denise shouldn't fear foreign currency fluctuations but instead should view investing in other countries and dealing with the ups and downs of currency as yet another form of investment diversification. More diversification can be good to further reduce risk of significant losses occurring in her overall portfolio.

Crunching the Numbers

Denise's Current RRSP Content:

LMN Cdn. Equity Fund	$4,000	100% RRSP eligible
RST Cdn. Bond Fund	$4,000	100% RRSP eligible
PQR International Equity Fund	$2,000	eligible as foreign content
Total portfolio	**$10,000**	80% Cdn., 20% foreign
Investment outside of Canada:		**20%**

Denise's possible RRSP content using synthetic funds (assuming she sold her current Cdn. equity fund and replaced it with a synthetic fund):

IND U.S. Synthetic Index Fund	$3,000	100% RRSP eligible
RST Cdn. Bond Fund	$5,000	100% RRSP eligible
PQR International Equity Fund	$2,000	eligible as foreign content
Total portfolio	**$10,000**	80% Cdn., 20% foreign
Investment outside of Canada:		**50%**

STRATEGY #45

Take Advantage of Your Employer's Pension Plan

Many Canadian employers offer some form of *pension plan* to their employees. A pension plan can be an effective forced savings plan to build retirement savings, where the employer may also contribute toward the plan. Employer contributions can be a great added bonus to boost savings, and these contributions are generally a non-taxable benefit.

From an investment point of view, many pension plans include investment options similar to those you could purchase outside the plan on your own. From a tax point of view, your contributions to an employer pension plan are tax deductible, just like your contributions to your *RRSP*. Contributions to a pension plan also affect your RRSP contribution room through something called a pension adjustment. The pension adjustment helps to ensure that an individual contributing to a pension and an RRSP does not have more tax-deferred contribution room compared to someone who has no pension plan and can contribute only to an RRSP. The pension adjustment is calculated by your employer and will reduce the amount you can contribute to your regular RRSP.

Deciding whether to contribute to your employer's pension plan — if you have a choice! — really depends on a variety of factors, including whether you think you can do better on your own with additional RRSP investments. Remember, having a pension plan reduces RRSP contribution room. Other financial factors to consider when deciding whether to join a pension plan include the amount of the employer's contribution to your plan, whether the employer's contributions will increase over time, fees, investment choices, and total pension benefits to be received in retirement versus total expected RRSP income. Like an RRSP, money in your pension plan will grow tax free during your working life, and won't be taxed until you start to receive payments from the plan, usually in retirement.

Aside from the financial considerations in deciding to contribute to a pension plan or an RRSP, there are several "human" factors that should be considered. Some people like the idea of a pension plan because it is a low-hassle investment process: during the working years it's a forced savings plan where someone else does all the investing, and in retirement you simply get a cheque at the end of each month. Some people who have RRSPs see their pension plan as added diversification of investments and access to professional *money managers* they otherwise could not use. And some people want to leave the investing and growth of their life savings up to full-time professionals and are content investing only a small RRSP on their own.

Deciding to get involved with your company's pension plan requires an examination of a variety of monetary and non-monetary factors. Weigh the importance of each in your own mind and evaluate the pros and cons of each option with an advisor who has no interest in selling you investment products (which might otherwise predispose the advisor to recommend the RRSP route).

▼

Example

Jenny just started a new job as a sales manager and has been looking over the employee benefits materials that arrived from the human resources department. She approached her financial advisor for advice about joining the company's defined contribution pension plan.

The advisor explained that a defined contribution plan is a plan where Jenny's pension income will be based on total contributions to the plan plus investment growth over time. The advisor pointed out that in addition to Jenny's own contributions, the employer will contribute an amount equal to 5% of her salary each year, and this could be a great boost to her savings. This employer contribution is valuable since without it Jenny would need to have that additional 5% capital from other sources just to match the pension plan contributions. These employer contributions may be lost, however, if Jenny decides to leave her employer before the employer contributions have *vested.*

In deciding whether to enrol in the plan, Jenny examined the following factors:

- She didn't know much about investing and didn't care to. Having someone else manage her money in the pension plan was appealing.
- She liked the additional contributions provided by the employer. That's money that wouldn't be there if she invested on her own.
- She was already managing her RRSP investments and didn't want to take on a greater personal time commitment. She felt she would just end up worrying about her money and likely couldn't do as well as professional money managers handling the pension funds.

- Her advisor examined the quality of the pension plan investments and managers and together agreed that the plan was being managed by large, established, and highly regarded pension fund managers with a long history of good results. Jenny liked the idea of dealing with a reputable institution that would likely be around for her lifetime and has a history of producing good results. She realized, though, that past results are not an indication of future results.
- Jenny realized that the professional pension managers were highly qualified people who invested and monitored her investments all day long, every day. She admitted that she could never consistently beat the efficiency and skill of these people. She was a bit concerned, however, that she had no control over the selection of money managers.
- Jenny was concerned about what would happen to her pension proceeds on death. She had an uncle who died five years after his retirement and his estate received nothing from the pension plan to which he had contributed for 35 years. Jenny and the financial advisor reviewed the plan details and were happy to learn that on Jenny's death her future spouse would be entitled to a reduced pension from Jenny's employer. Should Jenny never marry, her estate would be entitled to a lump sum.
- Jenny's last concern was about the long-term viability of her employer. What would happen if the company went *bankrupt*? The financial advisor pointed out that the pension plan proceeds were held by a third party, and in bankruptcy these funds would remain safe. The advisor pointed out that if the pension plan had been a defined benefit plan (where the employer guarantees a level of pension income and may be responsible for ensuring that the pension funds are adequate to meet this liability), there would be more of a concern if the employer wasn't keeping this plan fully funded.

The financial planner and Jenny together picked an investment mix of mutual funds available from the pension plan. Jenny completed the paperwork to have the contributions come right off her pay cheque, further simplifying the contribution process.

STRATEGY #46

Get Your Investment Advisor and Tax Accountant Working Together for You

Separately, neither your investment advisor nor your tax accountant may know enough to manage your wealth effectively, because each may not have the complete financial picture required to integrate planning strategies across investing goals, tax goals, and other goals you have. Together, these advisors have a greater ability to manage your entire financial situation and provide you with financial peace of mind.

Many investment advisors, much like mutual fund managers, are motivated to produce the highest gross return on investment, rather than the after-tax return that matters to you. Taxes have a significant impact on investment returns and investment strategies. Tax is an important variable, albeit only one of many variables that must be considered, in selecting the right investments for your *portfolio.* Keep in mind that the largest expenditure you may make in your lifetime will likely be the payment of income tax.

Understanding the intricacies of income taxes in Canada, one of the highest-taxed nations in the world, is a complex job. The leaders in tax expertise in Canada tend to be tax lawyers and tax chartered accountants who have completed the *CICA* In Depth Course. This formal training, supplemented by ongoing work experience and constant upgrading, is the minimum it takes to stay on the leading edge of Canadian taxation.

Now this is not to say that your investment advisor should necessarily be this highly tax trained, although there are some out there who are. However, you should consider the following suggestion: if you have a tax accountant who does your tax return, and if he or she is qualified, ask your accountant to get involved in consulting on the tax effectiveness of your investments and to generally assist you to "kick the tires" of new investment options.

Many of the larger investment brokerages in Canada have formal tax specialists on staff providing information to investment advisors about taxation. Your investment advisor likely has access to this information. But using it and understanding it are not the same. By asking some questions based on the content of this book, you may be able to tell if you are dealing with a competent tax advisor. If you are not, find one — and if you are looking for an investment advisor anyway, look for one with greater tax expertise, or one who recognizes his or her tax limitations and use outside advisors where necessary. Seeking advice from an investment advisor who claims to have a solid grasp on tax rules but lacks any formal training or experience can be dangerous. Of course, these same rules apply to searching for a tax accountant: seek advice from a tax accountant who is a properly qualified tax advisor.

Overall, making a team out of your investment advisor and tax accountant can be a very powerful tool toward wealth maximization.

▼

Example

Gina has a trading account with a *discount investment brokerage* and does her own trading. She admits she doesn't utilize "*tax-smart*" investing strategies, and has recently attended a seminar put on by a local investment advisor of a national brokerage firm. The investment advisor was accompanied by her firm's in-house C.A. and tax specialist. The seminar topic was tax-effective investing, and the investment advisor and C.A. together presented a thorough demonstration of their knowledge of investing and taxation. Gina liked the tax-effective approach to investing, and she decided to take up the investment advisor on her offer to provide a free evaluation of Gina's needs. Gina called the advisor to set up a meeting, and three days later they were sitting down at Gina's kitchen table.

Gina and her investment advisor chatted about the seminar, and the advisor explained that such seminars were presented twice a year for the purpose of educating clients and giving them a chance to pose questions to a professional with whom they might not regularly deal. This appealed to Gina, who was always looking for more financial education. She had been using a discount investment brokerage because although she had tried a *full-service* route before, she hadn't been able to find what she wanted in terms of an advisor relationship. She pressed the investment advisor for answers to the same concerns she had had before:

- Investing on an after-tax basis — The investment advisor stated that while tax considerations in investing are important, tax should be only one of many factors to consider for successful investing. And, tax should never be the most important factor. The investment advisor explained how together with the firm's in-house tax specialist, she utilizes effective tax-planning techniques on

Gina's behalf. She also encouraged Gina to have her recommendations validated by her own tax accountant.

- Charging fees based on money managed instead of transactions — The investment advisor described how for clients interested in one fee regardless of the number of transactions, her company offered products with fees based on annual market value of client investments. These products eliminate the concern that an investment advisor might be buying and selling frequently to generate *commissions* at the client's expense.
- Providing an annual rate of return — The investment advisor explained that she would be able to provide a *personal rate of return* on Gina's investments if she requested it, or the advisor could provide all the information to Gina's accountant if she wanted an independent person to calculate the return. The investment advisor explained that she believes knowing returns is important in order to show clients how well they have done in a year. Additionally, she believes that clients must also compare their returns to a relevant benchmark like the *TSE 300* or S&P 500, in order to know how well they have done. She includes the relevant benchmark with the rates of return that she provides.

Gina was ready to take the next step with this investment advisor, which according to the advisor would be letting her know Gina and her needs and objectives in detail. The investment advisor said the relationship would move at Gina's speed, and Gina promised to think about her needs and follow up.

STRATEGY #47

Contribute Equities as a Charitable Donation to Save Tax

Recently, the Minister of Finance has made significant improvements to the benefits related to charitable giving in Canada. Individuals are entitled to a non-refundable *tax credit* of 17% on the first $200 of donations, plus 29% on gifts made that are in excess of $200 (with even larger credits when you factor in related provincial tax credits). The maximum annual amount permissible for a tax credit is 75% of the individual's personal net income plus 25% of any *taxable capital gains* resulting from the charitable gifts and 25% of any *recapture* of *depreciation* arising from the donation of depreciable property such as an apartment block.

To encourage gifts of appreciated assets, the federal government recently reduced the income inclusion rate from 75% to 37.5% on capital gains arising from donations made after February 18, 1997, of certain property to charities. Eligible property includes shares of public companies, bonds, trust units, mutual funds, and some other investments. This means that if you make large charitable donations and also will sell investments to realize capital gains in the same year, you should consider giving the investments to a charity, to realize an overall tax saving.

And if you are deciding whether to contribute cash or mutual funds or another investment, consider your investment strategy before doing so. If you would otherwise hold a mutual fund that has grown in value as a long-term investment, a cash donation would likely be more tax effective. Donating the mutual fund would result in an early payment of tax on the mutual fund's accrued gain that otherwise could be deferred.

Here is another tip: remember how your federal tax credit is 17% on the first $200 of charitable donations, and then the credit rises to 29%? Well, it is in your best interest to try to get the 29% credit and achieve more tax-credit bang for your donation buck. Therefore, an individual and his or her spouse should consider claiming all their donations on one tax return each year, to ensure that they get over the $200 threshold. Couples currently claiming less than $200 on each of their tax returns may be losing out on an additional 12% federal tax credit (up to 20% combined federal-provincial) every year! You could also save donations for a few years in order to get over the threshold, because the donation credit is based on donations made in the current year and previous five years as long as the gifts haven't been claimed on a previous tax return.

Finally, consider timing your donations appropriately to take advantage of the higher tax credit. A $400 donation in one year compared to two $200 donations over two years can save you about $40.

▼

Example

Enzo lives a comfortable lifestyle and is thankful for all he has. He has a successful career, a wonderful family, and a large investment portfolio which he created himself through active investing. He is a believer in giving back to the community that helped him, and is in the habit of making sizable charitable donations to several charities each year. In the past, Enzo just wrote a cheque at the end of each year for all of his charitable contributions. He never thought about mixing his charitable contributions with his investments before. Rather, he kept his investment portfolio separate: he actively bought stocks and bonds, and simply sold something when he needed funds to finance living expenses. At year end, when he made his donations, he usually sold some of his short-term investments to cover the cash requirement.

Recently, Enzo was talking to his new tax accountant, Katie, about tax-planning opportunities. Enzo hired Katie to do a complete review of his tax situation to see if any planning opportunities were possible. Enzo had been doing his own taxes, and thought an independent professional review made sense. Katie spent some time going over Enzo's situation, and reported that he should consider making his annual charitable donations using stocks, rather than selling the stocks first and then contributing cash. Katie also confirmed with Enzo that this would be sensible because a number of his stock investments were ripe for sale in any case.

Crunching the Numbers

Katie described the benefits of this strategy as follows:

	Sell stocks and donate cash	**Donate stock**
Stock market value at sale date	$11,000	$11,000
Tax cost	$1,000	$1,000
Capital gain realized	$10,000	$10,000
Taxable gain included in personal income for the year	$7,500	$3,750
Tax on taxable gain (assume 50%)	($3,750)	($1,875)
Tax benefit of donation ($11,000 x 50% assuming all high rate)	$5,500	$5,500
Net tax benefit (tax benefit from credit less tax paid)	$1,750	$3,625
Tax savings from direct stock donation		**$1,875**

By donating stock instead of cash, Enzo can reduce his tax bill every year that he follows this strategy. The tax savings result because only 37.5% of the capital gain from the donation is included in income, as compared to the 75% income inclusion when the stock is sold personally.

STRATEGY #48

Evaluate Index-Linked GICs for Your Investment Strategy

More and more institutions are offering index-linked *GICs* for investors looking for more than the currently low returns available from traditional GICs. *Tax-smart* investors will notice that index-linked GICs may not be very attractive when owned outside an *RRSP* or *RRIF*. Here are some useful facts about these new products.

What Are Index-Linked GICs?

Index-linked GICs are investment products that combine the safety of a guaranteed investment certificate (GIC) with the investment return potential of an equity investment. An investor purchases a $5,000 GIC, for example, and receives a promise from the institution to get back at least the $5,000 at the end of the investment term. The potential rate of return on the GIC depends on the broader stock market index to which the GIC is tied (or linked). The extent to which the investor can earn the rate of return of the index (such as the TSE 100 index) will be set by the institution.

There are many varieties of index-linked GICs available.

They offer rates of return up to the potential returns of such indices as the TSE 100, S&P 500 in the U.S., and other internationally recognized indices.

What Are the Advantages of Index-Linked GICs?

- Index-linked GICs allow investors to share in the upside of the stock market but without taking on the risk of owning an equity investment. In recent times of low-interest GICs, this potential for higher returns has become attractive.
- The taxation of an index-linked GIC is usually deferred until the maturity of the investment. This is because the amount of the return on the investment will not be known until maturity, when the institution calculates the rate of return based on the change in the linked index.

What Are the Disadvantages of Index-Linked GICs?

- Many of the index-linked GICs available provide only a portion of the upside of the stock market. For example, if the TSE 100 does 30% next year, investors may get only 20%. Other products provide the average return over a period of time. Investigate the specific product at the institution you deal with, to understand the limitations.
- Index-linked GICs are *tax disadvantaged.* Since the potential return is only "index linked" and not an actual investment in an index investment, investors do not receive any of the dividends paid by the corporations in the indices. Receiving *dividends,* which are taxed at a much lower rate than *interest,* would be desirable to taxable investors. Dividends can also rise over time, providing a basic inflation fighter to an otherwise fixed income. Additionally, the return from the index link is taxed as *regular income* instead of as tax-advantaged

capital gains — as would be the case with a real index investment.

- There is some investment risk associated with an index-linked GIC, since when the investment matures you may receive only your original $5,000 principal back. No return may be guaranteed — as would be the case with a traditional GIC. And receiving no return means you've actually lost on your investment when you take inflation into account.
- The investment is a locked-in GIC which is not accessible until maturity. This does not provide flexibility.
- If the GIC permits you to look into a return during the term — say 20%, once the linked index reaches this level — you will be taxed on the accrued income when you lock in, even though you can't access the funds until maturity.

Who Are Index-Linked GICs Best Suited For?

These investments are more risky than traditional GICs (since no return may be guaranteed), but less risky than an outright investment in the stock market. They are suited for investors who want more potential return than GICs can offer, who can handle a bit of risk, but who aren't ready to deal with the potential loss of principal that could result from a direct investment in the stock market. Index-linked GICs are not suitable for someone who needs to live off annual income from the investment.

An investor's time frame is a key factor in deciding on these investments. Judging from history, investors will likely do better over the long term with a direct investment in the stock market than with an index-linked GIC. And why not receive dividends and capital gains instead of regular income? But in a short period of time (less than five years), the index-linked GIC may be more appropriate. If, for example, a couple are saving to buy a home in three years, they cannot afford a large drop in the stock market right before they plan to buy their home. Owning an index-linked GIC would prevent this from happening. But note that a zero return is also possible using index-linked GICs, if the stock market doesn't perform well.

Many elderly investors may be attracted to index-linked GICs because of the larger return potential. But buying an index-linked GIC (as a step toward investing in equities) should not be a substitute for appropriate *asset allocation* based on an analysis of risk/return for an investor. It may be more appropriate for seniors to invest their money in a 90% fixed income/10% equity portfolio that gives them tax advantages and inflation-fighting dividends than to buy an index-linked GIC that provides neither. And those seniors who need some investment income from their GICs should be aware that index-linked GICs may provide none at all if the stock market doesn't perform.

▼

Example 1

Antonio and Mary were recently married and want to use the cash gifts they received at their wedding to save for their first home. With their $35,000, they have enough for the initial deposit, but they want to make a larger deposit in order to reduce the mortgage. They expect to buy in about five years, and would like to invest the $35,000 in an investment that can only grow. In other words, they want protection of the $35,000, but they also want the ability to make more money.

Antonio and Mary met with their financial advisor, who explained to the couple that an index-linked GIC could be the appropriate type of investment for them at this stage: it would provide a guarantee of their existing capital, but with the upside potential to earn a double-digit stock market return, since the return of the GIC would be linked to the return of the S&P 500 Index in the United States. With a guarantee of principal, Antonio and Mary could rest assured that if the stock market dropped the day before they needed their money, their original $35,000 wouldn't be affected. Antonio and Mary also liked the fact that the investment would be locked in for five years, preventing them from spending the money on less important but tempting items in the meantime.

▼

Example 2

Ivan and his wife of 50 years, Katarina, were finding it harder and harder to live off their fixed incomes in their retirement. With interest rates so low lately, their investment income was far less than it was five years ago. All of their savings were invested in short-term GICs. On top of that, rising inflation continued to erode their purchasing power, so that their cash flow was buying less and less.

Although they were risk-averse investors, Ivan and Katarina went to their local financial institutions in search of new investments to increase their returns. An advisor introduced them to index-linked GICs and discussed how they offered the potential for above-average returns with no additional risk.

Ivan and Katarina listened closely, and then, armed with a handful of brochures, they decided to seek a second opinion about these investments. They proceeded to visit their other financial institution, and sat down with a second advisor. "Oh, but they do come with risk," the advisor said. "The two of you require an annual income from your GICs, so just getting a guarantee of principal is useless. You need an annual income, and because many index-linked GICs don't offer this feature, they are not the right type of investment for you.

"Instead, your GICs should be part of a more balanced portfolio of investments. Around your GICs we should build a portfolio of investments that includes bonds and bond mutual funds and some equities or equity mutual funds. Because of your risk averseness and inexperience with the investment marketplace, perhaps the level of equities in your portfolio should be 10% or less overall. But even with this small amount, you will get exposure to the stock market and have the possibility of earning significant returns. The dividends and capital gains earned from the equity investments will provide tax-advantaged income as compared to interest. The bonds and bond funds will generate annual interest income and are not locked in like a GIC. That means you can access your money whenever you want."

After the advisor took much more time to fully explain his recommendations, Ivan and Katarina agreed with his logic. They did need annual income. And their aversion to risk didn't mean that they couldn't handle a small amount of equity in their portfolio. Exactly how much equity would always be under their control, and that put them more at ease.

STRATEGY #49

Downsize Your Home in Retirement to Improve Your Cash Flow and Lifestyle

Here's something you might see: an elderly couple living on a small fixed pension and receiving some government benefits. They live a meagre fixed income lifestyle, getting by with few luxuries. This same couple is proud to state, however, that they own their home, the same home they've had for 40 years, and it is their pride and joy.

While there may be nothing wrong with this lifestyle, these seniors are asset rich and cash poor. Yes, they enjoy home ownership, but they may be sacrificing a more enjoyable day-to-day lifestyle in order to hang on to an oversized four-bedroom house. Keeping a large, valuable home because you "need the space when the kids visit one week a year" may mean you are giving up a lot in those other 51 weeks. This scenario is especially true in cities like Vancouver and Toronto where the value of homes has significantly increased in the last 30 years.

Seniors should consider *downsizing* their home as early as age 60. Downsizing may mean buying a smaller home, buying a condominium, or moving into an apartment, depending on personal preferences. If downsizing frees up even $100,000, this amount earning a basic 5% pre-tax can result in another $3,000 or so to the senior's after-tax income every year. That's a lot of money to seniors living on a small fixed income, and that money could enhance their lifestyle — maybe even pay for a vacation to see the kids!

Another nice thing about downsizing is that many of the things you enjoy about owning a home don't have to change if you simply buy a smaller home. But the boost to your cash flow will add to your daily lifestyle year after year.

This strategy can be applied to other valuable assets you own as a senior, such as antiques, art, or collectible stamps, for example. If you would love to visit your relatives across Canada every year but really can't afford it, consider selling the cottage you only use on long weekends and using the income from the invested proceeds to travel. You can always rent another cottage for a few weeks a year.

Take a long hard look at the assets you own as a senior, and determine if there are better uses for your money.

▼

Example

When Roger and Marg retired 10 years ago, they knew their fixed income pensions might force them to change their lifestyle. Since then, they have managed to fit their lifestyle into their income of $40,000 a year. But in the decade they have been retired, they have already noticed the impact that *inflation* has had on their standard of living. Their pensions are buying less and less each year.

Roger and Marg are hoping they can use their $190,000 in RRIFs to offset the inflation loss. With both of them at age 70 now, they realize this money may have to last another 25 years. With their home in Toronto paid off and no other debt, they think they can make it. They believe they'll just have to watch their spending.

When some of Roger's RRIF investments came due recently, they sat down with their *financial planner*, Chuck. He knows the financial situation of Roger and Marg well, and has already helped them to fight inflation by guiding them to buy some dividend-generating investments.

In their recent meeting, Chuck decided to make another suggestion. Roger and Marg would probably squeeze by financially in retirement, but they would never have the extra cash to enjoy a few more vacations, buy a new car, or even give a bit of money to their grandchildren. Chuck pointed out that the home Roger and Marg lived in was worth $380,000, growing at about 1% annually, and providing no income. They were asset rich, but cash-flow poor. Downsizing to a smaller home or condo could permit $200,000 to be invested which could produce annual before-tax income of $10,000 at a 5% rate of return. Cash flow for Marg and Roger could be even higher when the savings from lower property taxes and utilities are included. And because the home is their principal residence, the large capital gain realized on the sale would not be taxable!

Chuck also suggested that if Roger and Marg were prepared to rent, the full net-sale proceeds could be invested; this action could potentially cause their total family income to grow by 50% (pre-tax) from its current level, every year.

Roger and Marg were cool to the idea. They said their home was their castle and leaving it wouldn't be easy. But vacations and being able to afford pleasures like more golf were also important. They realized there was no rush to act, so they promised Chuck they would consider it.

STRATEGY #50

Measure Affordability of Life Insurance Before Buying

There is an opportunity to reduce taxes payable by your estate on death, by purchasing a life insurance policy that will pay out on your death so that the proceeds will offset the taxes due by your estate. Such a policy can be funded with regular payments while you are alive. While this can be an effective strategy to reduce the impact of taxes on death, there are issues that need to be addressed prior to a purchase of life insurance for this purpose.

- Can you afford the purchase of life insurance? If insurance premiums will significantly affect your cash flow while you are alive, and adversely affect your standard of living, is it sensible? Why buy life insurance and sacrifice your current lifestyle to enhance your heir's lifestyle after you have died? Senior citizens who are barely making ends meet on a fixed income should not be convinced that they need to pay *premiums* to purchase insurance just "so the kids will get a larger estate." These seniors may be sacrificing their own lifestyles by forcing themselves to live on less in order to afford the insurance premiums. And the kids may not need — or want — a larger estate. The kids would usually rather see you take the extra cash you have while you're alive and spend it on a vacation to come and visit them rather than applying it toward life insurance you may not be able to afford.

Purchasing life insurance to offset taxes on death can be an effective strategy in the appropriate situations. (See Strategy #43 on *universal life insurance.*) Evaluate your estate goals and the affordability of these goals prior to purchasing a policy. And seek a second opinion from a qualified advisor who is not selling you the policy and has no vested interest in making a sale to you.

Group Life Insurance

Many employees may have some amount of *group life insurance* offered through their employment. Similar insurance may also be offered by professional bodies, associations, and other organizations with members or employees. Be cautious not to rely too heavily on this insurance to meet all your needs for insurance. In some cases, you may be better off not buying the employer's group insurance for one or more of the following reasons: 1) if you pay premiums, they may be higher than if you had purchased insurance on your own, since the premiums factor in employees of all ages and health types; 2) with an employer's group policy, you may have little or no control over the type and amount of the policy; 3) your employer may be able to cancel the insurance at any time; 4) if you leave the employer, some or all of the insurance coverage may be lost.

Employer-provided group life insurance can be appropriate in the right circumstances, but a close evaluation of the policy should be made in order to understand coverage, benefits, and restrictions. If you need life insurance, shop around and purchase a policy that contains characteristics you need. Utilize a professional insurance advisor who understands what is important to you when purchasing insurance and who can provide access to a large variety of product options.

▼

Example

Shirley and Joe are having a great retirement. They saved aggressively throughout their working years, and now are enjoying having the financial freedom to afford the retirement they desire. They haven't had to cut back on their spending in retirement, and they can afford annual vacations, golf memberships, and spending time with their grandchildren. That's why they were a little confused when their insurance agent approached them about buying life insurance — they didn't know why they would need any.

The agent explained that the very fact that they were doing so well was the reason for his visit. He stated that as their *RRSP* manager, he noticed that their RRSPs had done very well and now contained in excess of $2 million dollars. This money would continue to provide ample cash flow to permit Shirley and Joe to live their desired lifestyle. They agreed. They also admitted that they can't even spend all the income they receive and are just reinvesting it again. And they said they expect this to continue as they have no expensive future plans.

The agent explained that on the death of the last survivor, the remaining RRSP or RRIF would be fully taxable at that time and taxed at approximately 50%. Any accrued capital gains that exist on their non-RRSP or RRIF investments will also be taxed at that time. When you add to this the probate costs, legal and accounting fees to wind up an estate, and even funeral costs, a substantial liability results on death. Taxes in particular can significantly reduce the size of an estate.

The agent suggested the purchase of a life insurance policy that would be funded by a series of payments. The policy would pay out on the death of the last survivor and would pay a tax-free benefit which could be used to cover the taxes and other expenses due on death.

The agent thinks that the policy is affordable for Shirley and Joe because they have excess cash flow to afford such a policy without affecting their lifestyle. It is also a good investment since the tax-free nature of the death benefit makes the insurance policy attractive as an investment. They may be hard pressed to invest the policy premium amounts and earn an equivalent rate of return in a taxable investment. Purchasing the policy may help to grow the value of their estate more than regular taxable investing. And having a large payout on death means that all the death taxes and other expenses on death could be offset by the insurance proceeds. This would leave a larger estate to the heirs.

Shirley and Joe agreed they had the surplus cash flow to afford such a life insurance policy. And the policy could always be cancelled if their finances worsened. They hadn't really thought before about maximizing their estate; they were prepared to give their kids whatever remained. However, if they could afford the insurance and it would serve to make their children more wealthy, they would consider it. They decided to think carefully about life insurance and seek a second opinion.

GLOSSARY

Commonly Used Financial Terms

Accrued Capital Gain — An unrealized gain that has been created by the increase in value of an investment or other asset. The excess of market value over adjusted cost base. An accrued gain is a gain that exists before the investment is sold, or deemed sold, to realize the gain.

Accrued Tax Liability — An unrealized tax liability relating to an accrued capital gain. The tax liability continues to accrue as the accrued capital gain increases. This liability will become taxes payable when the investment is eventually sold, or deemed sold, and the gain is realized.

Active Management — Management of, for example, mutual funds by professional money managers who actively buy and sell investments in an attempt to produce a greater rate of return than the market does. The opposite of passive management.

Adjusted Cost Base — The cost of an asset used in computing the capital gain or capital loss on disposition. The purchase price of an asset, plus or minus any adjustments under the Income Tax Act. Generally includes any transaction fees associated with the purchase and reinvested income and capital gains in mutual funds and pooled funds.

After-Tax Rate of Return — A measure of the profit retained from an investment over a period of time, after paying the related income tax. The rate of return is expressed as a percentage.

Allowable Capital Loss — See capital loss.

Annuity — An investment that guarantees a series of payments (often fixed) over a period of time. The amount of the payments can vary according to a number of variables, including interest rates, term, adjustments for inflation, and the price of the annuity.

Asset — Anything with value, either tangible or intangible, owned by an individual or a company. Examples: investments, real estate, vehicles, patents.

Asset Allocation Mix — The division of asset holdings among a variety of categories such as stocks or equity, bonds or fixed income, real estate, cash, etc. Determining a proper asset allocation mix for investing purposes can involve an assessment of one's risk tolerance, need for liquidity, and other factors to create an asset mix consistent with the investor's needs.

Asset Turnover — A measure of the rate of buying and selling of investments in an investment portfolio. Frequent buying and selling by a stock investment manager is high asset turnover.

Attribution Rules — Rules in the Income Tax Act of Canada designed to prevent transferring of investment income between family members for purposes of reducing income taxes paid on that income. The application of these rules results in the taxation of the income in the hands of the transferor.

Average Cost Base — An accounting of the cost of an asset where the owner holds a number of identical units. For example, if you buy 10 units at $20 each, the total cost is $200. If you purchase 10 more units at $30 each, their total cost is $300. You now have 20 units for a total cost of $500 and an average cost per unit of $25 ($500/20).

Bankrupt — The legal status of an insolvent person who has made an assignment of assets in favour of creditors or of a person against whom a receiving order has been made.

Beneficiary — An individual who is entitled to receive assets from a will, funds from a trust, the proceeds from an RRSP or RRIF, the proceeds from a life insurance policy, or some other form of receipt.

Blue Chip Stock — Stock in large, diversified, established companies that may be better able to weather a poor economy than smaller companies.

Bond — A financial contract between an issuer and holder where the issuer promises to pay interest to the holder at specified intervals and a fixed amount at maturity.

Bond Fund — See fixed income fund.

Broker — An investment advisor who is responsible for providing investment advice and executing buy and sell orders on behalf of clients.

Buy and Hold — An investment strategy of purchasing an investment with the intent to hold it for several years. The opposite of an investment strategy of frequent buying and selling.

C.A. — Chartered accountant. A Canadian professional accounting designation. One of the world's most recognized and highly regarded professional designations for advising on a broad array of personal and business issues. To become a C.A., one must complete advanced educational and experience requirements in accounting, tax, and auditing, among other topics.

Call Option — An option contract that gives a purchaser the right, but not the obligation, to purchase an investment at a fixed price up to point in time in the future.

Canadian Controlled Private Corporation (CCPC) — A Canadian corporation that is not controlled by non-residents or public companies or any combination of these types of shareholders. Usually these companies are owned and controlled by Canadian resident individuals or other CCPCs. Unlike a public company, a CCPC is not listed on a public stock exchange. Its stock does not trade publicly.

Canadian Resident — For Canadian income tax purposes, an individual who ordinarily resides in Canada (which is a question of fact), or has sojourned in Canada in a particular year by having spent 183 days or more in Canada in that year. A Canadian resident is taxed on his or her worldwide income. As it is possible to be a resident of Canada and another country at the same time under each country's respective tax law, Canada has entered into tax treaties with many countries to prevent double taxation by determining one country of residency and specifying in which of the countries the various sources of income may be taxed.

Canadian Shareholder's Association — An association that educates investors about investing and gives interested investors low-cost access to investing in companies in North America that permit direct stock purchases and dividend reinvestment.

Capital Gain — The excess of the sale proceeds of an asset over its adjusted cost base. A taxable capital gain is 75% of net capital gains (capital gains minus capital losses for the year). A taxable capital gain is the amount you include in income on your tax return. Throughout this book I refer to capital gains.

Capital Loss — The opposite of a capital gain. Seventy-five percent of net capital losses (capital losses minus capital gains) constitute an allowable capital loss. Net capital losses can only reduce taxable capital gains; they cannot otherwise reduce your income. An allowable capital loss can be deducted against past and future taxable capital gains. It can also be carried back up to three years or carried forward indefinitely to be applied against taxable capital gains in other years.

Capped Fund — A fund that is not accepting new investment money. The fund is said to be closed off to new investment.

Cash Position — A strategy in which professional money managers hold a portion of an investment portfolio in cash investments in order to take advantage of future buying opportunities. This is known as taking a cash position. The size of the cash position may vary significantly between managers.

CDIC — Canadian Deposit Insurance Corporation. An organization established by the federal government to provide a basic level of deposit insurance to Canadians invested with member institutions. Members include many of the major financial institutions in Canada. CDIC insurance covers bank accounts and GICs but not mutual funds.

C.F.P. — Certified financial planner. A professional designation offered by the Canadian Association of Financial Planners to individuals who have completed an educational requirement and achieved a level of experience in practising financial planning. The C.F.P. designation is becoming widely recognized as the designation of choice for financial planners in Canada.

CICA — Canadian Institute of Chartered Accountants, the national association of chartered accountants in Canada. A body that governs and educates chartered accountants in Canada and enforces a strict ethical code on their conduct.

Clone — A similar copy. To clone a mutual fund is to create a new mutual fund with similar, but not necessarily exactly the same, investment holdings and fees as the original fund. Cloned funds may have higher expenses.

Closed-End Trust — A trust with a fixed number of units for sale. Compare this with a mutual fund trust, which can offer an unlimited number of units for sale to investors as new money is invested with the fund company. Closed-end trust units are sold on a public stock exchange.

Collateral — Any assets pledged to support a debt. These assets may be sold to repay the debt if the borrower defaults on payments on the debt.

Commission — A broker's or agent's fee for executing a buy or sell order for investments owned by a client.

Common Shares or Stock — Stock, issued by a company, representing equity or ownership in the company. The purchaser of the stock is called a shareholder. Common stock usually has voting rights attached and may pay dividends.

Corporation — A legal entity, separate from its owners, through which an incorporated business is operated. A corporation is owned by shareholders. A corporation is also referred to as a company.

CPP — Canada Pension Plan. A retirement savings plan operated by the federal government of Canada. Working Canadians (employees and self-employed individuals) contribute to the plan and in retirement receive benefits in the form of regular payments.

Crystallization — The recognition for tax purposes of an increase in value of an investment without a sale. If you had an accrued gain in a stock on February 22, 1994, you were permitted to apply your remaining personal $100,000 capital gains exemption against some portion of this accrued gain, in effect crystallizing or realizing a gain for tax purposes and offsetting it with your exemption. The crystallized gain would have increased the cost base of the investment. Such a crystallization has a benefit when the stock is eventually sold, since any future gain should be smaller because of the higher cost base. A similar mechanism exists for mutual funds, whereby exempt capital gains balances, created by accrued capital gains in existence on February 22, 1994, can be used to offset future capital gains.

Deemed Disposition — A notional disposition (not a real sale) of an asset resulting in a realization of any accrued capital gains or losses and triggering any resulting tax. A deemed disposition occurs, for example, upon a death, when the deceased's assets are deemed to be disposed of at fair market value and tax may be due on any gains realized.

Deferral of Tax — The process of delaying the payment of tax until a point in the future. RRSPs and RRIFs defer tax since no tax is paid on income earned in the plan until the proceeds are withdrawn (usually in retirement). Deferral of tax is desirable because it permits assets to continue to earn income on a pre-tax basis, enhancing the growth rate.

Deferred Load — A deferred sales charge on mutual funds that occurs on the selling of the fund, rather than on its purchase. Also called a back-end load. Deferred loads or sales charges usually decrease to zero over a set period of years.

Depreciation — A notional charge against a capital asset to recognize that an asset's value is eroded with use over time. A non-cash expense that may be tax deductible (with very specific rules) for individuals and businesses. See also recaptured depreciation.

Derivative — A financial instrument that derives its value from another asset or investment such as an option or future contract. For example, an option contract to buy Coca Cola stock at a future date for a fixed price is a derivative. If the value of the stock goes up, so does the value of the option. On that future date, if the market price of Coke stock is greater than the option, the derivative holder can exercise the option, purchase Coke shares at the fixed price, then sell those shares at the higher market price, and profit on the difference. Or the holder could sell the option for a profit, since the value of the option would increase if the underlying stock could be purchased for a profit.

Disability Insurance — Insurance that protects against the loss of income of the insured individual because of illness or accident.

Discount Brokerage — An organization that sells financial products with lower fees than a full-service investment brokerage but provides little personal assistance and no advice to clients. Discount brokers assist clients to execute their transactions.

Disposition — The act of parting with something, whether it be a sale, gift, loss, or destruction. Also called disposal.

Distribution — Money allocated or directed to a unit holder of a mutual or pooled fund. A distribution may be interest, dividends, capital gains, or foreign income.

Diversification — The process of investing in a variety of countries, industries, and asset classes, across fixed income maturities and quality of debt, and across management styles in order to reduce risk of loss. A loss in one particular area would have a limited impact on the overall portfolio because of diversification.

Dividend — An after-tax corporate distribution paid to shareholders. Dividends may or may not be paid regularly, and the amount paid may vary. Dividends are generally subject to the lowest rate of tax on any type of investment income in Canada.

Dividend Reinvestment Plan — An arrangement whereby an owner reinvests dividend income for additional purchase of the original investment. Dividend reinvestment plans operate like compound interest and can permit much faster growth of investments because of the potential to earn income on income.

Downsizing — Moving from something larger to something smaller.

Earned Income — A term used for tax purposes that generally includes total income from employment and self-employment, alimony receipts, and rental income. Earned income is reduced by losses in self-employment, and rental losses. Earned income is important in determining RRSP contribution limits.

Emerging Market Bond — A bond offered by a second- or third-world country. Emerging market countries are countries that offer great opportunities (with greater risk) for development and industrialization and are eager to develop their economies.

Employment Income — Salary, wages, tips, gratuities, bonuses, and other benefits received in relation to a job. Annual employment income is reported to you on form T4, which is received from your employer each tax season.

Equity — Stock issued by a company, representing ownership in that company. See also stock; equity mutual fund.

Equity Mutual Fund — A mutual fund investing in equities or stocks of companies. There are several categories of equity mutual funds, including Canadian and international, among others.

Estate — The sum of the value of all an individual's property. All assets and liabilities owned by an individual at the time of his or her death.

Estate Freeze — The process of crystallizing the value of an individual's assets, typically the value of a business interest at its current market value, for tax purposes. This facilitates the transfer of future growth in the business at a low tax cost to other family members.

Estate Planning — The process of making legal and financial decisions relating to an individual's assets that will apply after death. Planning may involve preparing a will, creating a trust, implementing powers of attorney, and picking an estate executor, among other responsibilities.

Executor — A party named by an individual to carry out the provisions of his or her will.

Exempt Capital Gains Balance (ECGB) — A notional account representing the capital gain realized from the capital gains election made for flow through entities such as mutual funds. ECGB may have been created with the filing of your 1994 tax return. In that return you were permitted to create an account or pool consisting of the amount by which mutual fund market values exceeded the cost base on February 22, 1994. These accounts are available to reduce future capital gains distributed by the mutual fund or capital gains resulting from the sale of the mutual fund units, and effectively reduces any gains to zero for tax purposes, until the ECGB account is reduced to nil. ECGB accounts exist separately for each qualifying mutual fund.

Exercise — To assert a right in relation to a company stock option: to act on the option, advising the company that you would like to acquire the stock available from exercising the option.

Exercise Price — The price at which the owner of a stock option is entitled to purchase a share of the stock. Also called a strike price.

Face Value — The value of a bond that appears on its certificate. This is usually the amount to be received on maturity, excluding any interest income.

Fair Market Value — The amount that a buyer and seller would agree on in relation to the purchase and sale of an item, where the market is unrestricted and the buyer and seller are not connected in any way.

Financial Planner — A qualified individual who assists clients with the process of financial planning.

Financial Planning — A process of developing and prioritizing financial goals, and developing strategies to meet those goals. The process involves collecting information about a client's current personal and financial situation, identifying goals, developing alternatives and recommendations to meet goals, providing assistance with implementing goals, and monitoring the client's achievement of those goals over time.

Fixed Income Fund — A mutual fund that invests primarily in bonds, mortgages, and/or other forms of debt. Bond funds are a form of fixed income fund.

Foreign Content — The portion of an investment portfolio that is invested outside of Canada. For an individual's RRSP, the foreign content is restricted to 20% of the book value or cost.

Foreign Income — Income earned from sources outside of Canada. For tax purposes, foreign investment income including dividends (other than capital gains) is taxed as regular income.

Formal Trust — A legal relationship, evidenced by an agreement, created when a person (settlor) transfers property to another (trustee) who is responsible for dealing with the property for the benefit of persons known as beneficiaries. The fundamental characteristic of a trust is the separation of management of the property from entitlement to it. A trust is a separate taxpayer and must file a tax return annually.

Front-End Load — A fee paid on the purchase of a mutual fund. See also deferred load.

Full-Service Investment Advisor — An advisor that sells financial products and provides a broad array of financial advice and services to clients who don't have the time, knowledge, experience, or desire to select and manage their own investments.

Fund Company — A company, such as Templeton or Mackenzie, that offers mutual funds for sale. Mutual fund companies may also sell other services and products such as segregated money management or pooled funds.

Fund Manager — A professional money manager who is responsible for the selection and the timing of the buys and sells of investments in a portfolio. A fund manager can be an individual, a team of individuals, or a company.

Future — A contract that requires its owner to buy or sell a certain financial instrument at a stated price by a specified date.

GIC — Guaranteed Investment Certificate. A fixed income investment in which an investor deposits funds in an institution like a bank for a specified period of time and the institution pays the investor a fixed rate of return on the investment over that period. Principal is repaid to the investor at the end of that term. The investment return is in the form of interest income and the investment is usually locked in for its agreed term.

Global Diversification — The process of investing around the world to reduce the risk that significant loss in any one country would have a large impact on a portfolio of investments. See also diversification.

Group Life Insurance — Life insurance provided through an employer for an employee group. While this insurance can be quite inexpensive, the coverage may not suit your needs and may not be fully transferable if you leave the employer.

GST — Goods and Services Tax. A federal tax of 7% on the consumption of goods and services in Canada. The tax is collected by businesses on certain goods and services for sale.

Guaranteed Investment Certificate — See GIC.

Higher-Tax-Rate Income — Income that attracts a higher rate of tax depending on the taxpayer's marginal tax bracket.

Hot Fund — A fund for which the money manager has produced some very good returns recently or over the long term, compared to similar investments. See also star manager.

In Kind — As is. Transferring an investment whole, without selling it. Simply moving the existing investment to another institution or plan.

Income Tax Act of Canada — The federal statute that contains the income tax laws and regulations governing the taxation of individuals, corporations, and trusts in Canada. Such laws are created and amended federally by the minister of finance. Revenue Canada is the federal government department that administers the Income Tax Act and deals with Canadians and their federal taxes.

Index — A market indicator of broad market performance. In Canada, the Toronto Stock Exchange Composite Index (also called the TSE 300 Composite Index) includes stocks of 300 large and established Canadian companies.

Index Mutual Fund — A mutual fund that invests in the same securities included in a broad market index like the TSE 300 Composite in Canada or the Standard & Poor's 500 in the United States. This type of fund has no active fund manager since its holdings try to mirror the index and produce a rate of return similar to the index.

Inflation — A measure of the increase in cost of living over time. An example of the impact of inflation has been the rising price of a postage stamp over the years. As the cost of living increases through inflation, your income must also grow, in order to prevent a decrease in your standard of living through a loss of purchasing power.

Informal "In Trust" Account — An "in trust" arrangement offered by many Canadian financial institutions and investment brokerages, under which funds are held in trust by a parent (the trustee) for a child but a formal trust is not created and a trust tax return may not be filed.

Insolvent — Being unable to pay debts as they become due.

Interest — The cost of borrowing a sum of money or the benefit for lending a sum of money. Usually computed as a percentage rate over time.

International Equity Mutual Fund — A stock-based mutual fund that invests in the stock of companies based outside of Canada.

Investment Income — Income earned on passive investment of capital, such as interest, dividends, and capital gains. Investments can include stocks, bonds, GICs, mutual funds, rental properties, and pooled funds, among others.

Investment Risk — The risk that an investment will not provide the return expected, or that the investment will lose money.

Joint Ownership — Ownership of an asset by two or more people, where each person has an undivided interest in the property. Joint ownership can permit any owner to have access to the asset either on their own or together with the other joint owners.

Labour Fund — A labour-sponsored venture capital corporation, ("labour funds") offering yet another asset class for a diversified portfolio: venture capital. Labour funds, which operate much like mutual funds, have been approved by the federal and provincial governments for the purposes of making investments into private businesses in Canada.

Leverage — The act of borrowing money to invest.

Life Insurance — A financial safety net where under a policy contract you pay specified amounts (premiums) to an insurance company and in exchange the insurance company agrees to pay your estate or family a lump-sum amount when you die. The amount of your premiums is based on a number of variables, including how much insurance you want, your age, health condition, whether you smoke, your sex, etc. The policy payout is based on the terms of the policy and can be structured by the insurance company to be tax free when paid.

Line of Credit — An agreement under which a lender of money agrees to provide funds to a borrower as needed by the borrower, up to a fixed limit. The lender charges interest on the amount borrowed.

Liquidity — The ease with which an investment can be converted into cash.

Load — A transaction charge on the purchase or sale of units of a mutual fund. Loads can be front-end or deferred (or rear-end, also called deferred sales charges).

Locked-in Investment — An investment you are unable to convert into cash until a point in time agreed upon when the investment was purchased. GICs may be locked in for one year, for example.

Management Expense — A fee paid for the operation and administration of a mutual fund or other managed investment account. This is different from a load or a trailer, or a commission. The management fee for a mutual fund can include payment for the managers' salaries, advertising costs, and other administrative costs of operating the fund company and its funds.

Management Expense Ratio — A representation of all costs of operating a fund, including management expenses, expressed as a percentage of the net assets of the fund. For example, a typical Canadian equity mutual fund might charge a management expense ratio of around 2.25% annually.

Marginal Tax Rate — The tax rate that applies to the next dollar of taxable income you earn, given a specific taxable income level. Knowing your marginal tax rate for different types of income can permit you to organize your income sources to reduce tax paid.

Market Capitalization — A measure of the dollar value of a company. The total number of shares multiplied by the current price per share.

MER — See management expense ratio.

Money Manager — A person, group of people, or company that handles investments on behalf of others. The manager may buy or sell investments on behalf of the investors.

Money Market Instrument — A short-term fixed income investment. Examples include Treasury bills, GICs, money market mutual funds, and short-term bonds.

Mortgage — A legal contract, relating to a loan between a borrower and lender, where the lender receives the right to own pledged property if the borrower does not meet the conditions outlined in the loan agreement.

Mutual Fund — A professionally managed pool of investments owned by a group of investors. An investor can buy units in a fund and effectively invest in a wide range of stocks, bonds, and other investments that he or she might otherwise not be able to afford. Many funds are legally structured as trusts or corporations and the income earned by the fund each year is distributed to the unit holders after a fee is deducted for managing the fund. Investors can purchase mutual funds that invest in bonds, stocks, and other instruments in Canada and many other countries in the world.

Mutual Fund Corporation — A corporation set up by a mutual fund company, where different classes of shares are issued to represent investment in different types of mutual funds. Unit holders can switch among funds inside the corporation and not realize capital gains. But these funds are tax deferred, not tax exempt. This means that when the shares are eventually redeemed from the corporation, income tax will be due on the accumulated capital gains.

Natural Index Fund — A fund that replicates an index by purchasing the underlying investments that compose the index. For a Canadian equity index fund, the fund manager might purchase the stock of corporations included in the TSE 300 in the same proportion reflected in the index.

Net Asset Value — The value of one unit or share of a mutual fund. The total market value of all investments owned by a mutual fund, less all liabilities, divided by the number of units outstanding.

Net Capital Loss — See capital loss.

Net Worth — The difference between the value of an individual's total assets and his or her total liabilities. The improvement of an individual's net worth over time is a measure of success in personal finance.

No-Load Fund — A mutual fund that has no purchase or sale fees.

Non-Registered Investment — An investment that is not tax sheltered because it is held outside a registered plan such as a registered retirement savings plan or registered retirement income fund. Also called a non-RRSP/RRIF investment. Income from non-registered investments is subject to tax.

Notional Disposition — See deemed disposition.

Offshore Trust — A trust established and operated outside of Canada. See also formal trust.

Option Contract — An instrument representing the right to buy or sell an investment at an agreed-upon price known as the strike price. See also call option; put option.

Passive Management — Management that is associated with index mutual funds, where no professional money management is used but rather investments are purchased and sold to match the index that the fund is trying to mirror. The opposite of active management.

Pension Plan — A registered retirement plan sponsored by an employer for the benefit of employees. A pension plan is subject to government regulation and can be either a defined benefit plan or a defined contribution plan. Contributions to a pension plan may be made by employers and employees and are generally tax deductible. Growth inside the plan is tax sheltered until the benefits are paid out to a pensioner in retirement.

Performance — A measure of the success of an investment according to its increase in value and/or income generated over a period of time. Also called (percentage) rate of return on an investment. To calculate a percentage return on an investment over a year, divide the amount of income generated and the increase in investment value by the original cost of the investment and then multiply by 100.

Personal Rate of Return — A measure of the performance of an investment for the period of time that the investor owned the investment, instead of a period of time determined on some other basis like calendar year.

Pooled Fund — A fund investment similar to a mutual fund, except that in this case minimum investment amounts are $150,000 and MERs tend to be much lower than those of mutual funds. See also mutual fund.

Portfolio — The collection of investments held by an investor, whether registered or non-registered.

Premium — The purchase price of ownership of an amount of life insurance. Premiums can be paid in a lump sum or, more commonly, over a period of time.

Prescribed Annuity — An annuity that provides the beneficiary with a consistent stream of receipts over a future period of time. The payments consist of principal and interest. A prescribed annuity provides interest income evenly over the annuity's term, unlike a regular annuity which provides interest income in smaller amounts over the term of the annuity. A prescribed annuity serves to defer taxation better than a regular annuity because of the deferral of payment of interest over the life of the annuity.

Pre-Tax Return — A measure of the performance of an investment before related income tax is considered. Pretax or gross return is the return you see in the newspaper and what your advisor may report to you. These returns may or may not be after the payment of any fees, as well.

Probate Fee — A provincial fee, not a tax, for the processing or validation of a will for a deceased individual. Probate fees vary by province. They are calculated based on the value of assets in an estate.

Prospectus — A legal document outlining the key information about a particular investment. A prospectus is provided by the investment product offerer when the investment is offered for sale to the public. Prospectuses should be presented to and discussed with clients prior to the purchase of investments. Prospectuses for mutual funds contain information on fund fees, objectives, and administrative matters, among other things.

Public Corporation — A company whose stock is listed and traded on a public stock exchange in Canada. Because public stock is bought and sold on a public exchange, ownership can be more widely held and stock can usually be traded more easily.

Purchasing Power — A measure of the amount of goods and services that can be bought today with a given sum, compared to a prior or future period. A measure of how much a dollar buys over time. Purchasing power is eroded by inflation, which raises prices and reduces how much a dollar will buy.

Put Option — An option contract that gives a purchaser the right, but not the obligation, to sell an investment at a fixed price at a point in time in the future.

Real Estate Investment Trust (REIT) — A publicly traded closed-end trust that owns, operates, acquires, and develops or finances real estate properties.

Realization of a Gain — Receipt of the benefit of an increase in the value of an investment (gain) by its actual or deemed sale. Before the gain is realized, the gain is accruing on the investment. Capital gains are taxable only when they are realized, not when they are accruing.

Recapture — The difference between the lesser of the cost or sales price of a depreciable asset and the remaining tax cost (after depreciation). This difference is taxed as regular income. The excess of the sale price over the cost is taxed as a capital gain.

Redemption Charge — A fee charged to an investor for selling an investment within a predetermined time after the purchase. Also called a deferred load for mutual funds.

Registered Retirement Income Fund (RRIF) — An individual retirement account registered with the federal government. The assets have been transferred in from an RRSP or registered pension plan. Contributions cannot be made to a RRIF, and the annuitant must withdraw minimum sums from the RRIF each year according to government-determined amounts. Payments made out of the plan are taxable. Funds inside the RRIF can continue to be invested as desired and remain tax deferred until withdrawn. There are no maximum withdrawal amounts. An individual can convert an RRSP to a RRIF at any age up to but no later than the year in which he or she turns 69.

Registered Retirement Savings Plan — See RRSP.

Regular Income — Income other than investment income. Includes employment, business, and rental income. This is income that is not taxed at a preferred lower tax rate such as that applicable to dividends and capital gains. In Canada, foreign investment income may also be taxed as regular income.

REIT — See real estate investment trust.

Retiring allowance — A payment, for lengthy service or termination, for example, to an employee leaving an employer due to either retirement or forced early departure.

Revenue Canada — The federal government department that administers and enforces the laws contained in the Income Tax Act.

Risk/Return Balance — The trade-off between an individual's risk tolerance and his or her expected return on investment. Usually, the higher the potential rate of return, the higher the risk associated with getting this return.

Risk Tolerance — A measure of an individual's willingness or ability to endure risk — the possibility of a decline in the value of investments — in an attempt to obtain higher investment returns.

RRIF — See registered retirement income fund.

RRSP — Registered retirement savings plan. A savings or investment plan registered with the federal government of Canada. Contributions to RRSPs are based on limits determined with reference to earned income and benefits accruing under employer-sponsored registered pension plans and deferred profit-sharing plans. Contributions are tax deductible, and income inside the plan grows tax deferred. Individuals can contribute to their own RRSP or to a spousal RRSP. With a spousal RRSP, the contributor gets the tax deduction and the spouse withdraws the investment at least three years in the future and pays tax on the withdrawals at that time.

RRSP Contribution — An amount of money or the value of an asset deposited in an RRSP. The deposit amount is limited (as discussed under RRSP). An individual's contribution may not necessarily match the tax deduction for the year; the individual can contribute to an RRSP and defer taking the tax deduction until the future.

Segregated Money Management — The management of an investor's money and portfolio separate from other investors, where each investor owns their own portfolio of stocks and bonds. This differs from the situation in a mutual fund, where investors own units in a pool and never own individual securities.

Self-Employment Income — Income earned through an unincorporated business or professional practice. A doctor or lawyer in private practice usually earns self-employment income.

Share — A representation of ownership or equity of a company or corporation. See also stock.

Share Purchase Program — An agreement whereby a company offers investors the opportunity to purchase additional stock directly from the company.

Sole Proprietorship — An unincorporated business owned by one person. An unincorporated business is not separate from its owner and therefore there is no need to file a separate tax return for the business. Rather, the net income of the business is included on the tax return of the owner.

Star Manager — A mutual fund manager or other professional money manager who is very good at managing money and producing above-average rates of returns for investors over a period of time.

Stock — A representation of equity ownership of a company or corporation. Stock can be common or preferred. Each type of stock has different rights attached, such as voting ability and dividend entitlement.

Stock Exchange — A marketplace for buying and selling investments. A place where stock of public companies is listed and traded. Examples of stock exchanges include the Toronto Stock Exchange and the New York Stock Exchange.

Stock Option — A financial instrument given to an employee that permits the employee to purchase company shares at a specified price (exercise price) within a specified time period.

Strike Price — See exercise price.

Stripped Bond — A bond from which the interest payments ("coupons") have been removed. The remaining residue is then sold at a discount to its face value and matures at face value. The coupons are also sold at a discount to maturity value. The term "stripped bond" has come to reflect both the residual bond and the coupon payments.

Synthetic Index Fund — A fund that may use derivatives to purchase exposure to a particular index. A synthetic fund may use a futures contract to provide investors with a rate of return equal to the change in the index.

Tax Bracket — A specified range of taxable income to which a given tax rate applies. In Canada, tax rates are progressive; that is, the rate of tax generally increases as income increases.

Tax Compliance — The process of reporting tax information required by statute, including completing a tax return. This differs from tax planning, which provides strategies to save and defer tax.

Tax Credit — An amount that is applied directly to reduce the amount of tax owing by an individual, trust, or company in preparing its tax return. This differs from a tax deduction, which reduces the amount of income that is subject to tax.

Tax Deduction — A deduction from the amount of income that is subject to tax, resulting in a reduction of the amount of tax owing by an individual, trust, or company.

Tax Instalment — The amount of tax remitted by a taxpayer to Revenue Canada on a quarterly basis (in the case of individuals). Individuals are required to make tax instalments if they earn a large amount of income from which no tax is withheld at source. Tax instalments can be calculated according to three methods, and the method most appropriate to you should be determined.

Tax Planning — The process of developing tax-saving and tax-deferral strategies for individuals, trusts, and companies, within the rules of the Income Tax Act of Canada.

Tax Shelter — An investment intended to provide investors with a deferral or reduction of tax.

Tax Smart — Tax effective, or giving consideration to deferring or minimizing tax.

Taxable Capital Gain — The portion of a capital gain that is included in your income for tax purposes. The taxable portion is 75% of the net capital gains.

Taxable Income — The amount of income that is subject to tax after all permitted tax deductions have been made. The relevant tax rate is applied to taxable income.

Tax-Advantaged Income — The opposite of tax-disadvantaged income.

Tax-Deferred Growth — Investment growth that attracts no current taxation. Tax-deferred growth occurs inside tax-sheltered plans like registered pension plans, RRSPs, or RRIFs. Accruing capital gains on investments also grow tax deferred until realized. Tax-deferred growth means that tax will be paid on this investment when it is eventually sold or removed from its tax-sheltered protection.

Tax-Disadvantaged Income — Investment income that is subject to a higher rate of tax than other types of investment income. The opposite of tax-advantaged income. Interest income and employment income are tax disadvantaged since they generally attract a higher tax rate than dividends and capital gains.

Term Certain Annuity — An annuity that provides a stream of payments to an investor for a fixed period of time; as opposed to a life annuity, which provides payments for the life of the annuitant.

TIPS — TSE 35 Index Participation units. These units are created by the Toronto Stock Exchange to permit investors to own a piece of the TSE 35 Index, which consists of some of the largest and most heavily traded publicly listed companies in Canada, and is a subset of the TSE 300. Ownership of the TSE 35 offers diversification geographically and across industries; it offers liquidity, as the units are easy to sell; and it offers the flow-through of dividend payments paid by the companies owned by the units. Most of the 35 companies included in the TIPS index have a market capitalization greater than $1 billion.

Tracking error — The difference between the performance of an index and the performance of a mutual fund that is attempting to mirror that index, when the fund company doesn't buy and sell the appropriate investments at exactly the same time that the index's components change. Fund returns are also decreased by fees to the fund company to manage the fund and pay the operating costs.

Trailer Fee — A fee paid to an investment advisor by a mutual fund company when one of its funds has been purchased through that advisor. The investment advisor may receive trailer fees as long as the advisor is used by the client to hold his or her investments. The trailer pays for ongoing service provided to the client by the advisor.

Treasury Bill — Short-term debt issued by the federal and some provincial governments at a discount, to mature at face value. There is no interest paid; rather, the difference between the purchase price and maturing value is taxed as interest income.

Trust — See formal trust.

Trustee — The administrator of a trust.

TSE 300 Composite Index — A Canadian index of public company stocks representing 300 of the largest companies in Canada trading on the Toronto Stock Exchange. The TSE 300 is widely used as a measure of the performance of the stock market in Canada.

T3 Slip — A federal government form used to report income and capital gains received from owning an interest in a trust (including a mutual fund trust). Income and capital gains reported on a T3 slip should be reported on your personal tax return in the year received.

Undervalued Investment — An investment that is selling for less than it is thought to be worth, based on the company's net assets and performance.

Unit — A measure of ownership of an open-ended mutual

fund. Units are bought and sold to reflect ownership in the fund. The unit value fluctuates with the increases and decreases in value of the investments inside the fund.

Unit Holder — An owner of units in a mutual fund.

Universal Life Insurance — A form of permanent life insurance where the insurance component and the savings element are separate and distinct, and the policy owner may have several investment options to consider for the savings part of the policy, along with flexibility on the timing and amount of premium deposits.

Unrealized Gain — The opposite of a realized gain.

Vesting — The right to keep one's benefits that have been created by an employer's contributions to a pension plan. Before contributions are vested, an employee may lose all employer-contributed benefits to his or her pension if he or she leaves the employer. The benefits of resting also apply to stock options.

Wrapped Investment Account or Product — An investment for which professional money managers have been contracted to manage pieces of the investment portfolio. A wrapped product might consist of mutual funds, pooled funds, or segregated money management. All fees are combined into one that is charged to the investor. Wrapped products thus provide access to multiple money managers through one source.

Yield — The amount of return generated by an investment, expressed as a percentage. Dividend yields for stocks are calculated by dividing the annual dividend by the current market price of the stock. Bond yields factor interest payments together with the difference between purchase price and face value and maturity date.

Would you like a checklist of all 50 strategies to use on your clients or yourself?

If you sell financial services, you may find it useful to have a one-page checklist of the 50 strategies which you can apply to your clients' personal situations to ensure that they are taking advantage of these strategies.

If you are interested in receiving a free strategy template (which you can personalize and copy) in the form of a checklist, send your name, address, and a self-addressed envelope to Kurt Rosentreter at the address below.

▼

Tax- and financial-planning speaking engagements and personal counselling for you, your family, and your clients

Kurt Rosentreter regularly speaks publicly on personal finance, tax strategies, and wealth management. He is also available for personal consultations to develop an investment or personal tax plan or to address any other issues of personal financial planning for you and your family.

Contact Kurt Rosentreter directly by email at Kurt.Rosentreter@ca.eyi.com or by mail at Box 251, 222 Bay Street, Toronto, Canada, M5K 1J7 for more information. You can also visit Kurt Rosentreter's website at http://objectiveadvisor.com